**Follow the Scriptures of the blood
- the red scarlet thread -
that runs through the Bible.**

Dr. Gene Schuyler

Scarlet Thread of Redemption

Copyright © 2013 by Gene Schuyler

First Printing 2013

All rights reserved. No part of this publication may be reproduced, stored in a

Retrieval system or transmitted in any form by any means, electronic,

Mechanical, photocopy, recording or otherwise without prior permission of the publisher, except as provided by USA copyright law.

ISBN: 978-0-615-90845-8

Scripture quotations are from the King James Version of the Bible unless otherwise stated.

Printed in the United States of America

Cover photo: Gene Schuyler

DEDICATION

This book is dedicated to the faithful members of Mid-Way Baptist Church of Raleigh, North Carolina, who for ten weeks sat through these messages hour after hour on Sunday night, never complaining about the time we spent in this study nor the depth of this subject.

Their increase of wanting to know what the Scriptures teach us was the driving force that kept me more in the Word of God in this subject than I have ever spent in my entire forty-five years of ministry.

A special thanks to the ushers of our church that made sure that everyone received their notes at every service, and even went beyond their service to have more copies made as needed.

Acknowledgment

I want to thank Mrs. Judy Naylor, a dear and wonderful Christian lady of our church who read the first manuscript and helped work on this project with her expertise and to make this statement, "I pray that many will purchase "THE SCARLET THREAD," read it and allow God to minister to them and revive their heart also."

Thanks "Miss Judy."

Table of Contents

Dedication .... *v*

Acknowledgment .... *vi*

Introduction .... *viii*

Chapter 1
Redemption by Blood 9

Chapter 2
What the Bible Teaches About the Blood of Christ 24

Chapter 3
Reconciliation through the Blood 39

Chapter 4
Cleansing through the Blood 51

Chapter 5
Sanctification through the Blood 64

Chapter 6
There is life in the Blood 80

Chapter 7
Victory through the Blood 97

Chapter 8
Joy In Heaven through the Blood 109

Chapter 9
Living in "The Holiest" through the Blood 121

Introduction

In Joshua 2:1-21, we read a very vital passage of Scripture that has a great deal to do with this series of messages.

Dr. Criswell comments on the scarlet-colored blood-red thread that Rahab hung out of her window, "The scarlet line of Rahab is a symbol of her faith that God will provide deliverance in the time of judgment. Throughout the Bible 'scarlet' speaks of sacrifice made on the behalf of the believer, and it is seen in the vestments of the tabernacle and in the priestly garments in Exodus." This series of messages is not based on Dr. Criswell's famous sermon, "The Scarlet Thread of Redemption," but my basic idea came from it.

Rahab was saved from destruction because she had enough faith in God to hang a red rope out of her window. This blood-red rope is a type or picture of the blood-red scarlet thread that runs through the Bible, from Genesis to Revelation. The Schofield note on Joshua 2:21 says, "The scarlet line of Rahab speaks, by its color, of safety through sacrifice (Hebrews 9:19, 22)." That red rope pictures the scarlet thread that runs from one end of the Bible to the other.

This book contains my notes along with some revisions of the sessions with the Mid-Way Baptist Church family on Sunday evenings.

CHAPTER ONE

Redemption by The Blood

I Peter 1:18-19

The Scarlet Thread

The shedding of His blood was the culmination of the sufferings of our Lord. The atoning efficacy of those sufferings was in that shed blood. It is therefore of great importance that the believer should not rest satisfied with the mere acceptance of the blessed truth that he is redeemed by that blood, but should press on to a fuller knowledge of what is meant by that statement, and to learn what that blood is intended to do in a surrendered soul.

Its effects are manifold, for we read in Scripture of RECONCILIATION through the blood; CLEANSING through the blood; SANCTIFICATION through the blood; UNION WITH GOD through the blood; VICTORY over Satan through the blood; LIFE through the blood.

These are separate blessings but are all included in one sentence: REDEMPTION BY THE BLOOD.

Chapter One

It is only when the believer understands what these blessings are, and by what means they may become his, that he can experience the full power of REDEMPTION.

Before passing on to consider in detail these several blessings let us first inquire, in a more general way, concerning THE POWER OF THE BLOOD OF JESUS.

First, WHERE DOES THE POWER OF THAT BLOOD LIE?

Secondly, WHAT HAS THAT POWER ACCOMPLISHED?

Thirdly, HOW DOES THIS POWER WORK?

I. WHERE DOES THE POWER OF THAT BLOOD LIE?

What is it that gives to the blood of Jesus such power? How is it that in the blood, alone, there is power possessed by nothing else?

The answer to this question is found in Leviticus 17:11. "The life of the flesh is in the blood" and I have given it to you upon the altar to make an atonement for your souls, for it is the blood that maketh an atonement for the soul."

It is because the soul, or life, is in the blood, and that the blood is offered to God on the altar, that it has in it redemptive power.

The soul or life is in the blood; therefore, the value of the blood corresponds to the value of the life that is in it.

The life of a sheep or goat is of less value than the life of an ox; and so, the blood of a sheep or a goat in an offering is of less value than the blood of an ox (Leviticus 4:3, 24, 27). So then, the life of man is more valuable than that of many sheep or oxen.

The Scarlet Thread

And now, who can tell the value or the power of the blood of Jesus? In that blood, dwelt the soul of the holy Son of God. The eternal life of the Godhead was carried in that blood (Acts 20:28).

The power of that blood in its diver's effects is nothing less than the eternal power of God Himself. What a glorious thought for everyone who desires to experience the full power of the blood.

But the power of the blood lies above everything else in the fact that it is offered to God on the altar for redemption.

When we think of blood as shed, we think of death; death follows, when the blood or the soul is poured out. Death makes us think of sin, for death is the punishment of sin. God gave Israel the blood on the altar, as the atonement or covering for sin; that means - the sins of the transgressor were laid on the victim and its death was reckoned as the death or punishment for the sins laid upon it.

The blood was thus the life given up to death for the satisfaction of the law of God, and in obedience to His command. Sin was so entirely covered and atoned for, it was no longer reckoned as that of the transgressor. He was forgiven.

But all these sacrifices and offerings were only types, and shadows, till the Lord Jesus came. His blood was the reality to which these types pointed.

His blood was in itself of infinite value, because it carried His soul or life. But the atoning virtue of His blood was infinite also, because of the manner in which it was shed. In holy obedience to the Father's will, He subjected Himself to the penalty of the broken law, by pouring out His soul unto death. By that death, not only was the penalty borne, but the law was satisfied, and the Father glorified. His blood atoned for sin, and thus made it powerless. It has a marvelous

Chapter One

power for removing sin, and opening heaven for the sinner; whom it cleanses, sanctifies, and makes meet for heaven.

It is because of the Wonderful Person whose blood was shed; and because of the wonderful way in which it was shed, fulfilling the law of God, while satisfying its just demands, that the blood of Jesus has such wonderful power. It is the blood of Atonement, and hence has such efficacy to redeem; accomplishing everything for, and in, the sinner, that is necessary for salvation.

II. WHAT HAS THAT POWER ACCOMPLISHED?

As we see something of the wonders that power has accomplished, we shall be encouraged to believe that it can do the same for us. Our best plan is to note how the Scriptures glory in the great things which have taken place through the power of the blood of Jesus.

> ### THE BLOOD OF JESUS HAS OPENED THE GRAVE.

We read in Hebrews 13:20, "Now the God of peace, that brought again from the dead our Lord Jesus that great Shepherd of the sheep, THROUGH THE BLOOD OF THE EVERLASTING COVENANT."

It was through the virtue of the blood that God raised up Jesus from the dead. God's almighty power was not exerted to raise Jesus from the dead, apart from the blood.

He came to earth as surety, and bearer, of the sin of mankind. It was through the shedding of His blood alone that He had the right, as man, to rise again, and to obtain eternal life through resurrection. His blood had satisfied the law and righteousness of God. By so doing He had overcome the power of sin, and brought it to naught. So also, death was defeated as its sting, sin, had been removed; and the devil also was defeated, who had the power of death, having now lost all right over Him and us. His blood had destroyed the power of death, the devil and hell--THE BLOOD OF JESUS HAS OPENED THE GRAVE. He, who truly believes that, perceives the close connection which exists between the blood and the almighty power of God. It is only through the blood that God exerts His almightiness in dealing with sinful men. Where the blood is, there the resurrection power of God gives entrance into eternal life. The blood has made a complete end of all the power of death, and hell; its effects surpass all human thought.

> **Again, THE BLOOD OF JESUS HAS OPENED HEAVEN.**

We read in Hebrews 9:13, Christ "by His own blood He entered in once into the holy place, having obtained eternal redemption for us."

We know that in the Old Testament Tabernacle, God's manifested presence was inside the veil. No power of man could remove that veil. The High Priest alone could enter there, but only with blood, or the loss of his own life. That was a picture of the power of sin in the flesh, which separates us from God. The eternal righteousness of God guarded the entrance to the Most Holy Place that no flesh might approach Him.

But now our Lord appears, not in a material, but in the true Temple. As High Priest and representative of His People, He asks for Himself, and for sinful children of Adam, an entrance into the presence of the Holy One. "That where I am, there they may be also" is His request. He asks that heaven may be opened for each one, even for the greatest sinner, who believes in Him. His request is granted. But how is that? It is through the BLOOD. He entered THROUGH HIS OWN BLOOD. THE BLOOD OF JESUS HAS OPENED HEAVEN.

Chapter One

So it is ever, and always, through the blood that the throne of grace remains settled in heaven. In the midst of the seven great realities of heaven (Hebrews 12: 22, 24), yes, nearest to God the judge of all, and to Jesus the Mediator, the Holy Spirit gives a prominent place to "THE BLOOD OF SPRINKLING."

It is the constant "speaking" of that blood that keeps heaven open for sinners, and sends streams of blessing down on earth. It is through that blood that Jesus, as Mediator, carries on without ceasing, His mediatorial work. The Throne of grace owes its existence ever, and always, to the power of that blood.

Oh, the wonderful power of the blood of Christ! Just as it has broken open the gates of the grave and of hell, to let Jesus out, and us with Him; so it has opened the gates of heaven for Him and us with Him, to enter. The blood has an almighty power over the kingdom of darkness, and hell beneath; and over the kingdom of heaven, and its glory above.

> ➤ **THE BLOOD OF JESUS IS ALL POWERFUL IN THE HUMAN HEART.**

Since it avails so powerfully with God and over Satan, does it not avail even more powerfully with man, for whose sake it was actually shed? We may be sure of it.

The wonderful power of the blood is especially manifested on behalf of sinners on earth. Our text is but one out of many places in Scripture where this is emphasized. "Ye were redeemed from your vain conversation with the precious blood of Christ" (I Peter 1:18-19).

The Scarlet Thread

The word REDEEMED has a depth of meaning. It indicates particularly deliverance from slavery by emancipation or purchase. The sinner is enslaved, under the hostile power of Satan, the curse of the Law, and sin.

Now it is proclaimed "ye are redeemed through the blood," which had paid the debt of guilt, and destroyed the power of Satan, the curse, and sin.

Where this proclamation is heard and received, there Redemption begins, in a true deliverance from a vain manner of life, from a life of sin. The word "REDEMPTION" includes everything God does for a sinner from the pardon of sin, in which it begins (Ephesians 1:14; 4:30), to the full deliverances of the body by Resurrection (Romans 4:24).

Those to whom Peter wrote of were, "Elect…to the sprinkling of the blood of Jesus Christ." It was the proclamation about the precious blood that had touched their hearts, and brought them to repentance; awakening faith in them, and filling their souls with life and joy. Each believer was an illustration of the wonderful power of the blood.

Later on, when Peter exhorts them to holiness, it is still the precious blood which is his encouragement; on that he would fix their eyes.

For the Jew, in his self-righteousness, and hatred of Christ; for the heathen, in his godliness, there was only one means of deliverance from the power of sin. It is still the one power that affects daily deliverance for sinners. How could it be otherwise? The blood that availed so powerfully in heaven and over hell IS ALL-POWERFUL, ALSO IN A SINNER'S HEART. It is impossible for us to think too highly, or to expect too much, from the power of Jesus' blood.

Chapter One

III. HOW DOES THIS POWER WORK?

In what conditions and under what circumstances can that power secure, unhindered, in us, the mighty results it is intended to produce?

The first answer is, that just as it is everywhere in the kingdom of God,

> **IT IS THROUGH FAITH.**

But faith is largely dependent on knowledge. If knowledge of what the blood can accomplish is imperfect, faith expects little, and the more powerful effects of the blood are impossible. Many Christians think that if now, through faith in the blood, they have received the assurance of the pardon of their sins; they have a sufficient knowledge of its effects.

They have no idea that the words of God, like God Himself, are inexhaustible; that they have a wealth of meaning and blessing that surpasses all understanding.

Too often we do not remember that when the Holy Spirit speaks of cleansing through the blood, such words are only the imperfect human expressions of the effects and experiences by which the blood, in an unspeakably glorious manner, will reveal its heavenly life-giving power to the soul.

As we seek to find out what the Scripture teaches about the blood, we shall see that faith in the blood, even as we now understand it, can produce in us greater results than we have yet known, and in the future a ceaseless blessing may be ours.

The Scarlet Thread

Our faith may be strengthened by noticing what the blood has already accomplished. Heaven and hell bear witness to that. Faith will grow by exercising confidence in the fathomless fullness of the promises of God. Let us heartily expect that as we enter more deeply into the fountain, its cleansing, quickening, and life giving power, will be revealed more blessedly.

We know that in bathing we enter into the most intimate relationship with the water, giving ourselves up to its cleansing effects. The blood of Jesus is described as a "fountain opened for sin and uncleanness" (Zechariah 13:1). By the power of the Holy Spirit it streams through the heavenly Temple. By faith I place myself in closest touch with this heavenly stream, I yield myself to it, I let it cover me, and go through me. I bathe in the fountain. It cannot withhold its cleansing and strengthening power. I must, in simple faith, turn away from what is seen to plunge into that spiritual fountain which represents the Savior's blood, with the assurance that it will manifest its blessed power in me.

So let us with childlike, persevering, expectant faith, open our souls to an ever increasing experience of the wonderful power of the blood.

But there is still another reply to the question as to what else is necessary, that the blood may manifest its power.

Scripture connects the blood most closely with the Spirit. It is only where the Spirit works that the power of the blood will be manifested. This now brings us to this thought.

> **THE SPIRIT AND THE BLOOD.**

We read in First John that, "there are three that bear witness in earth, the Spirit, and the water, and the blood: and these three are one" (I John 5:8).

Chapter One

The water refers to baptism unto repentance and the laying aside of sin. The blood witnesses to redemption in Christ. The Spirit is He who supplies power to the water and the blood. So also, the Spirit and the blood are associated in Hebrews 9:14, where we read, "How much more shall the blood of Christ, who through the eternal Spirit offered himself without spot to God, purge your conscience." It was by the eternal Spirit in our Lord, that His blood had its value and power.

It is always through the Spirit that the blood possesses its living power in heaven, and in the hearts of men.

The blood and the Spirit ever bears testimony together. Where the blood is honored in faith or preaching, there the Spirit works; and where He works, He always leads souls to the blood. The Holy Spirit could not be given till the blood was shed. The living bond between the Spirit and the blood cannot be broken.

It should be seriously noticed, that if the full power of the blood is to be manifested in our souls, we must place ourselves under the teaching of the Holy Spirit.

We must firmly believe that He is in us and is carrying on His work in our hearts. We must live as those who know that the Spirit of God really dwells within, as a seed of life, and He will bring to perfection the hidden, powerful effects, of the blood. We must allow Him to lead us. Through the Spirit the blood will cleanse, sanctify and unite us to God.

When the Apostle desired to arouse believers to hearken to God's voice, with His call to holiness, "Be ye holy, for I am holy," he reminded them that they had been redeemed by the precious blood of Christ.

The Scarlet Thread

➢ **KNOWLEDGE NECESSARY.**

The Christian must know that they have been redeemed, and what that redemption signified, but we must above all know that "it was not by corruptible things such as silver and gold," things in which there was no power of life, "but by the precious blood of Christ."

For us to have a correct perception of what the preciousness of that blood is, as the power of a perfect redemption, would be to us the power of a new and holy life.

This same truth concerns us that are saved also. We must know that we are redeemed by the precious blood. We must know about redemption and the blood before we can experience its power.

In proportion as we more fully understand what redemption is, and what the power and preciousness of the blood are, by which redemption has been obtained, we shall the more fully experience its value.

➢ **NEED AND DESIRE.**

First: A deeper sense of need and a desire to understand the blood better. The blood has been shed to take away sin. The power of the blood is to bring to naught the power of sin.

Today, if we are not careful, we become too easily satisfied with the first beginnings of deliverance from sin.

May we no longer be satisfied with the fact that we, as redeemed ones, sin against God's will in so many things.

It should be the desire that holiness in our everyday living become stronger in us. Should not the thought that the blood has more power than we

Chapter One

know of, and can do for us greater things than we have yet experienced, cause our hearts to go out in strong desire? If there were more desire for deliverance from sin, for holiness and intimate friendship with a Holy God, it would be the first thing that is needful for being led further into the knowledge of what the blood can do.

As we inquire from the Word, in faith, what the blood has accomplished, it must be a settled matter with us that the blood can manifest its full power also in us. No sense of unworthiness, or of ignorance, or of helplessness must cause us to doubt. The blood works in the surrendered soul with a ceaseless power of life. The challenge is that we surrender ourselves to God the Holy Spirit.

The blood, on which the Throne of Grace in heaven is founded, can make your heart the temple and throne of God.

The Scarlet Thread

SELAH!
THINK ON THESE THINGS

"It is because of the Wonderful Person whose blood was shed; and because of the wonderful way in which it was shed, fulfilling the law of God, while satisfying it's just demands, that the blood of Jesus has such wonderful power. It is the shed blood of Atonement and hence has such efficacy to redeem; accomplishing everything for, and in, the sinner, that is necessary to salvation."

Read again Hebrews 9:13 and rejoice of this passage of Scripture.

Where this proclamation is heard and received, there Redemption begins, in a true deliverance from a vain manner of life; the sinner is enslaved under the hostile power of Satan the curse of the law and sin. The word "REDEMPTION" includes everything God does for a sinner from the pardon of sin, in which it begins, to the full deliverance of the body by Resurrection.

Take time now and reflect on your salvation and write a love note to your Savior:

_____
_____
_____
_____

Chapter One

So let us with childlike, persevering, expectant faith, open our souls to an ever increasing experience of the wonderful power of the blood.

CHAPTER TWO

What The Bible Teaches

About the Blood of Christ

Hebrews 9:20-22

Chapter Two

If there is anything that Satan hates, it is the blood of the Lord Jesus Christ. Satan knows that if the blood of Jesus was not shed for man's sin, he would have conquered this world.

From Genesis to Revelation, the Word of God speaks of the precious blood of Jesus. Calvary was the heart and mind of God way before He created this world. All through the Old Testament we find the prophecy of the blood. God was showing us the consequence for sin is death, and that there was no way man could approach Him without the shedding of blood (Romans 6:23).

Dr. Bailey Smith, who has preached at Mid-Way Baptist Church a few years ago, gave us four basic reasons why people are offended when they hear about Christ's death on the cross:

> One: The cross appears to be defeat when it is actually victory!

The Scarlet Thread

<u>Two</u>: The cross appears to be the wrong way.

<u>Third</u>: The cross appears to be death. It only seems to be death when in actuality it is the embodiment of eternal life for all those who embrace Jesus Christ by faith.

<u>Fourth</u>: The cross appears to be the end. The cross began a new mission, a new ministry, and a new might.

So, this is why our text verses for this chapter are found in Hebrews 9:20-22. Why? Because God wants us to know that there is a "dynamic," wonderful power in the blood of the LAMB.

In this chapter I will show you, by God's leadership, how to understand what the blood does:

1. The Blood redeems (I Peter 1:18-19)

2. The Blood brings us near (Ephesians 2:13)

3. The Blood cleanses (I John 1:7)

4. The Blood gives power over Satan (Revelation 12:11)

It is my desire, to introduce you to what the Scriptures teach us concerning THE GLORIOUS POWER OF THE BLOOD OF JESUS, and the wonderful blessings provided for us by it. I cannot lay a better foundation for this series of lessons nor give a better proof of the superlative glory of THAT BLOOD AS THE POWER OF REDEMPTION, than to have you follow me through the Bible, and thus see the unique place which is given to THE BLOOD from the beginning to the end of God's revelation of Himself to man, as recorded in the Bible.

Chapter Two

Please understand that in no way, will I be able to do complete justice to all this subject covers. I will give you enough that it will give you a greater understanding of this FUNDAMENTAL subject of God's Word that is so important to every Christian.

It will become clear that there is no single scriptural idea, from Genesis to Revelation, more constantly and more prominently kept in view, than that expressed by the words - "THE BLOOD."

Our study then is what the Scriptures teach us about THE BLOOD.

First, IN THE OLD TESTAMENT;

Secondly, IN THE TEACHING OF OUR LORD JESUS HIMSELF;

Thirdly, IN WHAT THE APOSTLES TEACH; and

Lastly, WHAT JOHN TELLS US OF IT IN REVELATION.

I. WHAT DOES THE OLD TESTAMENT TEACH?
The record about THE BLOOD begins at the gates of Eden.

At this time, I will not go into the unrevealed mysteries of Eden, but in connection with the sacrifice of Abel all is plain. He brought of "the firstlings of his flock" to the Lord as a sacrifice, and there, in connection with the first act of worship recorded in the Bible, blood was shed. We learn from Hebrews 11: 4, that it was "by faith" Abel offered an acceptable sacrifice, and his name stands first in the record of those whom the Bible calls "believers." He had this witness borne to him "that he pleased God." His faith, and God's good pleasure in him, is closely connected with the sacrificial blood.

The Scarlet Thread

In the light of later revelation of this testimony, given at the very beginning of human history, is of deep significance. It shows that there can be no approach to God; no fellowship with Him by faith; no enjoyment of His favor, apart from THE BLOOD.

Scripture gives us little of the following sixteen centuries, then came THE FLOOD, which was God's judgment on sin by the destruction of the world of mankind.

Then God brought forth a new earth from that awful baptism of water. Notice, however, that the new earth must be baptized also with blood, and the first recorded act of Noah, after he had left the ark, was the offering of a burnt sacrifice to God. As with Abel, so with Noah a new beginning, it was "NOT WITHOUT BLOOD."

Sin once again prevailed, and God laid an entirely new foundation for the establishment of His Kingdom on earth.

By the divine call of Abram, and the miraculous birth of Isaac, God undertook the formation of a people to serve Him. But this purpose was not accomplished apart from the shedding of THE BLOOD. This is apparent in the most solemn hour of Abraham's life.

God had already entered into a covenant relationship with Abraham, and his faith had already been severely tried, and had stood the test. It was reckoned, or counted to him, for righteousness. Yet he must learn that Isaac, the son of promise who belonged wholly to God, can be truly surrendered to God only by death.

Chapter Two

Isaac must die. For Abraham, as well as for Isaac, only by death could freedom from the self-life be obtained. Abraham must offer Isaac on the altar.

Four hundred years pass, and Isaac has become, in Egypt, the people of Israel. Through her deliverance from Egyptian bondage, Israel was to be recognized as God's first-born among the nations. Here also, it is "NOT WITHOUT BLOOD." Neither the electing grace of God, nor His covenant with Abraham, nor the exercise of His omnipotence which could so easily have destroyed their oppressors, could dispense with the necessity of THE BLOOD.

What THE BLOOD accomplished for one person (when Isaac was offered up by Abraham), who was the Father of the nation, must now be experienced by that nation. By the sprinkling of the door frames of the Israelites with the BLOOD of the Paschal lamb; by the institution of the Passover as an enduring ordinance with the words "When I see the BLOOD I will pass over you," the people were taught that life can be obtained only by the death of a substitute. Life was possible for them only through THE BLOOD of a life given in their place, and appropriated by "the sprinkling of that blood."

It was in that BLOOD the Covenant had its foundation and power. It is by THE BLOOD alone, that God and man can be brought into covenant fellowship. That which bad been foreshadowed at the Gate of Eden, on Mount Ararat, on Mount Moriah, and in Egypt was now confirmed at the foot of Sinai, in a most solemn manner. Without BLOOD, there could be no access by sinful man to a Holy God.

There is, however, a marked difference between the manner of applying the blood in the former cases as compared with the latter. On

The Scarlet Thread

Mount Moriah the life was redeemed by the shedding of the blood. In Egypt it was sprinkled on the door posts of the houses; but at Sinai, it was sprinkled on the persons themselves. The contact was closer, the application more powerful.

If you look further, you will be told that always, and for everything, THE BLOOD is the one thing needful. At the consecration of the House, or of the Priests; at the birth of a child; in the deepest penitence on account of sin; in the highest festival; always, and in everything, the way to fellowship with God is through THE BLOOD alone.

This continued for fifteen hundred years. At Sinai, in the desert, at Shiloh, in the Temple on Mount Moriah, it continued till our Lord came to make an end of all shadows by bringing in the substance, and establishing a fellowship with the Holy One, in spirit and truth.

II. WHAT OUR LORD JESUS HIMSELF TEACHES ABOUT THE BLOOD.

With His coming old things passed away, and all things became new. He came from the Father in Heaven, and can tell us in divine words the way to the Father.

It is sometimes said that the words "NOT WITHOUT BLOOD" belong to the Old Testament. But what does our Lord Jesus Christ say? Notice that when John the Baptist announced His coming, he spoke of Him as filling a dual office, as "THE LAMB OF GOD that taketh away the sin of the world;" and then as "the One who would baptize with the Holy Spirit." The outpouring of the BLOOD of the Lamb of God must take place before the outpouring of the Spirit could be bestowed. Only when all that the Old Testament taught about THE BLOOD has been fulfilled, can the Dispensation of the Spirit begin.

Chapter Two

The Lord Jesus Christ Himself plainly declared that His death on the Cross was the purpose for which He came into the world; that it was the necessary condition of the redemption and life which He came to bring. He clearly states that in connection with His death the shedding of His BLOOD was necessary.

In the Synagogue at Capernaum Christ spoke of Himself as "THE BREAD OF LIFE;" of His flesh, "that He would give it for the life of the world." Four times over He said most emphatically, "Except ye . . . drink this BLOOD, ye have no life in you." "He that drinketh my BLOOD hath everlasting life." "My BLOOD is drink indeed." "He that drinketh my BLOOD dwelleth in me and I in him." Our Lord declared the fundamental fact that He Himself, as the Son of the Father came to restore to us our lost life, can do this in no other way than by dying for us; by shedding His blood for us; and then making us partakers of its power.

Our Lord confirmed the teaching of the Old Testament Offerings - that man can live only through the death of another, and thus obtain a life that through Resurrection has become eternal.

But Christ Himself cannot make us partakers of that eternal life which He has achieved for us, save by the shedding of His blood, and causing us to drink it. This we will discuss in more detail in chapter six. Marvelous fact!

Jesus gave us the truth on the last night of His earthly life, before He completed the great work of His life by giving it "as a ransom for many," He instituted the Lord's Supper saying, "And He took to cup and gave thanks, and gave it to them, saying, drink ye all of it; for this is MY BLOOD of the New Testament, which is shed for many for the remission of sins" (Matthew 26:27-28). Without the shedding of blood there is no remission of sins; without remission of sins there is no life. But by the shedding of His BLOOD He has obtained a new life for us. By what He calls *"the drinking of His blood"*, He shares His life with us. The blood SHED in the Atonement which frees us from the SIN, the guilt of sin; and from death, the punishment of sin; the blood, which by faith we drink bestows on us His life. The BLOOD He shed was, in the first place FOR us, and is then given TO us.

III. THE TEACHING OF THE APOSTLES UNDER THE INSPIRATION OF THE HOLY SPIRIT.

After His Resurrection and Ascension, our Lord is no longer known by the Apostles "after the flesh." Now, all that was symbolic has passed away, and the deep spiritual truths expressed by symbol, are unveiled.

Even though there is no veiling of THE BLOOD, it still occupies a prominent place in the Christian doctrine.

Hebrews chapter nine was written purposely to show that the Temple service had become unprofitable and was intended by God to pass away now that Christ had come.

Here, if anywhere, it might be expected that the Holy Spirit would emphasize the true spirituality of God's purpose, yet it is here that the Blood of Jesus is spoken of in a manner that imparts a new value to the phrase.

By such words the Holy Spirit teaches us that the blood is really the central power of our entire redemption. "NOT WITHOUT BLOOD" is as valid in the New Testament as in the Old.

We must remember and continue to proclaim that nothing but the Blood of Jesus, shed in His death for sin, can cover sin on God's side, or remove it on ours.

Chapter Two

We find the same teaching in the writings of the Apostles. Paul writes of "being justified freely by his grace through the redemption that is in Christ Jesus . . . . through faith in his blood" (Romans 3:24-25).

To the church at Corinth, Paul declares that the "cup of blessing which we bless, is the communion of the Blood of Christ" (I Corinthians 10:16).

In the church at Galatia, he uses the word "CROSS" to convey the same meaning; while in Colossians, he united the two words and speaks of "The Blood of His Cross" (Galatians 6:14; Colossians 1:20).

He reminds us in Ephesians that, "We have redemption through his blood" and that we "are made nigh by the blood of Christ" (Ephesians 1:7; 2:13).

We find Peter reminding his readers that they were, "Elect . . . unto obedience and sprinkling of the Blood of Jesus" (I Peter 1:2), that they were redeemed by "the precious blood of Christ" (I Peter 1:19).

See how John assures his "little children" that, "The blood of Jesus Christ his Son cleanseth us from all sin" (I John 1:7). The Son is He "who came not by water only but by water and blood" (I John 5:6).

Through these scriptures we see that all of them agree in mentioning the blood, and in glorying in it, as the power by which eternal redemption through Christ is fully accomplished, and is then applied by the Holy Spirit.

IV. WHAT DO WE LEARN FROM THE BOOK OF REVELATION CONCERNING THE FUTURE GLORY OF THE CHURCH AND THE BLOOD?

It is of the greatest importance to notice that in the revelation which God has given in this book, the glory of His throne, and the blessedness of those who surround it, the blood still retains its remarkably prominent place.

The Scarlet Thread

Later on when He saw the great company which no man could number, He was told in reply to His question as to who they were, "They have washed their robes, and made them white in the blood of the Lamb." There is a question here for us. Can you not see that it is not difficult to see what lessons the Lord wishes us to learn from the fact that the blood occupies such a prominent place in Scripture, and the need for the church to take a strong stand?

> **GOD HAS NO OTHER WAY OF DEALING WITH SIN, OR THE SINNER, SAVE THROUGH THE BLOOD.**

For victory over sin and the deliverance of the sinner, God has no other means or thought than "THE BLOOD OF CHRIST." Yes, it is indeed something that surpasses all understanding.

> **THE BLOOD MUST HAVE THE SAME PLACE IN OUR HEARTS WHICH IT HAS WITH GOD.**

From the beginning of God's dealings with man, from before the foundation of the world, the heart of God has rejoiced in that blood. Our heart will never rest, nor find salvation, until we too learn to walk, and glory in the power of that blood.

> **LET US TAKE TIME AND TROUBLE TO LEARN THE FULL BLESSING AND POWER OF THAT BLOOD.**

The blood of Jesus is and will be the greatest mystery of eternity and the deepest mystery of the divine wisdom. This truth cannot be easily grasped in its meaning and we must take time, if we are to ever gain knowledge of the power of the blood.

Chapter Two

It is vital to understand that the:

- Sacrificial blood always meant the offering of a life. The Israelite could not obtain blood for the pardon of his sin, unless the life of something that belonged to him was offered in sacrifice.

- The Lord Jesus did not offer up His own life, and shed His blood to spare us from the sacrifice of our lives. No, but to make the sacrifice of our lives possible and desirable.

- The hidden value of His blood is the spirit of self-sacrifice, and where the blood really touches the heart, it works out in that heart, a like spirit of self-sacrifice. We learn to give up ourselves and our lives as to press into the full power of that new life, which Christ's blood has provided for us.

- We give our time so that we may become acquainted with these things by God's Word.

- We are to separate ourselves from sin and worldly-mindedness, and self-will, that the power of the blood may not be hindered, for it is these things that the blood seeks to remove from our lives.

- We surrender ourselves wholly to God in prayer and faith, so that we do not think that our own thoughts, and not to hold our own lives as a prize, but as possessing nothing save what Christ bestows. Then He reveals to us the glorious and blessed life which has been prepared for us by the blood.

The Scarlet Thread

➢ **WE CAN RELY UPON THE LORD JESUS TO REVEAL TO US THE POWER OF HIS BLOOD.**

It is by this confident that we are to trust in Christ and that the blessing obtained by the blood becomes ours. We must never, in thought, separate the blood from the High Priest who shed it, and ever lives to apply it.

- He who once gave His blood for us, will, so surely, every moment, impart its efficacy.

- Trust Him to open your eyes, and to give you a deeper spiritual insight.

- Trust Him to teach you to think about the blood as God thinks about it.

- Trust Him to impart to you, and to make effective in you, all that He enables you to see.

- Trust Him above all, in the power of His eternal High Priesthood, that He will work out in you, unceasingly, the full merits of His blood, so that your whole life may be an uninterrupted abiding in the sanctuary of God's presence.

Dear Christian, listen to the moving invitation of your Lord - - Come nearer. Let Him teach you; let Him bless you. Let Him cause His blood to become to you spirit, life, power, and truth.

Why not begin now, as you complete this chapter, to open your soul in faith, to receive the full, by faith the mighty, heavenly effects of the precious blood, in a more wonderful way than you have ever experienced. He Himself will work these things out in your life.

Chapter Two

SELAH!
THINK ON THESE THINGS

Why it is that Satan hates the blood of The Lord Jesus Christ?

In this chapter, you found out how to understand what the blood does. Can you recall them?

1. _____

2. _____

3. _____

4. _____

What lessons did you learn that The Lord wishes us see, that the blood occupies such a prominent place in Scripture and the need for the church to take a strong stand?

1. _____

2. _____

3. _____

4. _____

The Scarlet Thread

The Blood Redeems

The Blood Brings Us Near

The Blood Cleanses

The Blood Gives Power Over Satan

CHAPTER THREE

Reconciliation Through The Blood

Romans 3:24-25

The Scarlet Thread

As we have seen, several distinct blessings have been procured for us by the power of the blood of Jesus, which are all included in the one word "REDEMPTION." Among these blessings, RECONCILIATION takes the first place. The reason for this is that it stands first among the things the sinner has to do, who desires to have a share in REDEMPTION. Through it, a participation in the other blessings of Redemption is made possible.

To us, the believer who has already received RECONCILIATION should obtain a deeper and more spiritual conception of its meaning, and blessings. If the power of the blood in REDEMPTION is rooted in RECONCILIATION, then a fuller knowledge of that RECONCILIATION is the surest way to obtain a fuller experience of the power of the blood. The heart that is surrendered to the teaching of the Holy Spirit will surely learn what RECONCILIATION means, so then for us to understand what RECONCILIATION BY THE BLOOD means, we must first see.

I. SIN, WHICH MADE RECONCILIATION NECESSARY.

In all the work of Christ, and above all in RECONCILIATION, God's object is the removal and destruction of sin. Knowledge of sin is necessary for the knowledge of RECONCILIATION.

We need to understand what there is in sin that needs RECONCILIATION, and how RECONCILIATION renders sin powerless. Then faith will have something to take hold of, and the experience of that blessing is made possible to us.

Chapter Three

Sin has had a twofold effect. It has had an effect on God, as well as on man. We emphasize generally its effect on man. But the effect it has exercised on God is more terrible and serious. It is because of its effect on God that sin has its power over us. God, as Lord of all, could not overlook sin. It is His unalterable law that sin must bring forth sorrow and death (James 1:15). When man fell into sin, he, by that law of God, was brought under the power of sin. So it is with the plan of God that REDEMPTION must begin, for if sin is powerless against God, and the law of God gives sin no authority over us, then its power over us is destroyed and that it has no longer authority over us.

So then, what was the, effect of sin upon God? It was in His divine nature, He ever remains unchanged, and unchangeable, but in His relationship and bearing towards man, an entire change has taken place.

- ➢ **SIN IS DISOBEDIENCE, CONTEMPT OF THE AUTHORITY OF GOD;**

- ➢ **SIN SEEKS TO ROB GOD OF HIS HONOR, AS GOD AND LORD;**

- ➢ **SIN IS A DETERMINED OPPOSITION TO A HOLY GOD. IT NOT ONLY CAN, BUT WILL AWAKEN GOD'S WRATH.**

While it was God's desire to continue in love and friendship with man, sin has compelled Him to become an opponent. Although the love of God towards man remains unchanged, sin made it impossible for Him to admit man into fellowship with Himself. It has compelled God to pour out upon man His wrath and punishment, instead of His love. The change which sin has caused in God's relationship to man is awful.

The Scarlet Thread

Man is guilty before God - Guilt is debt. We know what debt is. It is something that one person can demand from another, a claim which must be met and settled.

When sin is committed its after-effects may not be noticed, but its guilt remains. The sinner is guilty. God cannot disregard His own demand that sin must be punished; and His glory, which has been dishonored, must be upheld.

As long as the debt is not discharged, or the guilt put to an end, it is, in the nature of the case, impossible for a Holy God to allow the sinner to come into His presence!

I like what one author said of this subject: "We often think that the great question for us is, how we can be delivered from the indwelling power of sin; but that is a question of less importance than, how can we be delivered from the guilt which is heaped up before God? Can the guilt of sin be removed? Can the effect of sin upon God, in awakening His wrath, be removed? Can sin be blotted out before God? If these things can be done, the power of sin will be broken in us also. It is only through RECONCILIATION that the guilt of sin can be removed."

The word "RECONCILIATION" means actually "to cover." Even heathen people had an idea of this, but in Israel God revealed a RECONCILIATION which could so truly cover and remove the guilt of sin, that the original relationship between God and man can be entirely restored. This is what true RECONCILIATION must do. It must so remove the guilt of sin, that is, the effect of sin on God, that man can draw near to God, in the blessed assurance that there is not any longer any guilt resting on him to keep him away from God.

Chapter Three

II. THE HOLINESS OF GOD WHICH FORE ORDAINED THE RECONCILIATION.

This must also be considered if we are to understand RECONCILIATION correctly.

God's Holiness is His infinite, glorious perfection, which leads Him always to desire what is good in others as well as in Himself - He bestows, and works out what is good in others, and hates and condemns all that is opposed to what is good.

In His holiness, both the LOVE and WRATH of God are united. Let me explain it this way - His LOVE which bestows itself; HIS WRATH which, according to the divine law of righteousness, casts out and consumes what is evil.

It is, as the Holy One, that God ordained RECONCILIATION in Israel, and took up His abode on the Mercy Seat.

It is, as the Holy One, that He, in expectation of New Testament times, said so often, "I am thy Redeemer, the Holy One of Israel."

Not only have we seen that RECONCILIATION means COVERING. It means that something else has taken the place where sin was established, so that sin can no longer be seen by God.

But because God is the Holy One, and His eyes as a flame of fire, that which covered sin must be something of such a nature that it really counteracted the evil that sin had done, and also that it so blotted out sin before God that it was really destroyed, and was not now to be seen.

The Scarlet Thread

RECONCILIATION for sin can take place only by satisfaction and satisfaction is RECONCILIATION. As satisfaction is through a substitute, sin can be punished, and the sinner saved. God's holiness also would be glorified, and its demands met, as well as the demand of God's love in the redemption of the sinner, and the demand of His righteousness in the maintenance of the glory of God and of His law.

We know how this was set forth in the Old Testament laws of the offerings. A clean beast took the place of a guilty man. His sin was laid, by confession, on the head of the victim, which bore the punishment by surrendering its life unto death. Then the blood, representing a clean life that now through the bearing of punishment is free from guilt, can be brought into God's presence; the blood or life of the beast that has borne the punishment in place of the sinner. That blood made RECONCILIATION, and covered the sinner and his sin, because it had taken his place, and atoned for his sin.

There was RECONCILIATION IN THE BLOOD, but we must remember, that was not a reality. The blood of cattle or of goats could never take away sin; it was only a shadow, a picture, of the real RECONCILIATION. Blood of a totally different character was necessary for an effectual covering of man's guilt. So then, based on the counsel of our God, nothing less than the blood of God's own Son could bring about RECONCILIATION. Righteousness demanded it; love offered it. "Being justified freely by his grace through the redemption that is in Christ Jesus whom God hath set forth to be a propitiation through faith in His Blood, to declare His righteousness for the remission of sins that are past, through the forbearance of God;" (Romans 4:24-25).

Chapter Three

**III.	THE BLOOD THAT WROUGHT OUT THE RECONCILIATION.**

RECONCILIATION must be the satisfaction of the demands of God's Holy Law.

The Lord Jesus accomplished that by a willing, and perfect obedience. He fulfilled the law under which He had placed Himself. In the same spirit of complete surrender to the will of the Father, He bore the curse which the law had pronounced against sin. He rendered, in fullest measure of obedience or punishment, all that the law of God could ever ask or desire. The law was perfectly satisfied by Him. So then how can Christ's fulfilling of the demands of the law be RECONCILIATION for the sins of others? Because, both in Creation and in the holy covenant of grace that the Father had made with Him, He was recognized as the head of the human race. Because of this, He was able, by becoming flesh, to become a second Adam. When ***He, the WORD, became FLESH,*** He placed Himself in a real fellowship with our flesh which was under the power of sin, and He assumed the responsibility for all that sin had done in the flesh against God. His obedience and perfection was not merely that of one man among others, but that of Him who had placed Himself in fellowship with all other men, and who had taken their sin upon Himself.

Above all, we must never forget that He was God. This bestowed a divine power on Him, to unite Himself with His creatures, and to take them up into Himself. It bestowed on His sufferings a virtue of infinite holiness and power. It made the merit of His blood-shedding more than sufficient to deal with all the guilt of human sin. It made His blood such a real RECONCILIATION, such a perfect covering of sin, that

The Scarlet Thread

the holiness of God no longer beholds it. It has been, in truth, blotted out. The Blood of Jesus, God's Son, has purchased a real, perfect and eternal RECONCILIATION.

The Righteousness of God no longer terrifies man for it now meets him as a friend, with an offer of complete justification. God's countenance beams with pleasure and approval as the penitent sinner draws near to Him, and He invites him to intimate fellowship. He opens for him a treasure of blessing. There is nothing now that can ever separate him from God (John 10:28-30).

The RECONCILIATION through the blood of Jesus has covered our (those that are born again) sins; they appear no longer in God's sight. He no longer imputes sin. RECONCILIATION has wrought out a perfect and eternal redemption.

It is no wonder that forever mention will be made of that blood in the song of the redeemed, and through all eternity, as long as heaven lasts, the praise of the blood will resound. But here is the wonder that the redeemed on earth do not more heartily join in that song and that they are not abounding in praise for the RECONCILIATION that the power of the Blood has accomplished.

IV. THE PARDON WHICH FOLLOWS FROM RECONCILIATION.

The fact that the blood has made RECONCILIATION for sin, and covered it, and that as a result of this a wonderful change has taken place in the heavenly realms - all this will avail us nothing, unless we obtain a personal share in it. It is in the pardon of sin this takes place.

Chapter Three

God has offered a perfect acquittal from all our sin and guilt. Because RECONCILIATION has been made for sin, we can now be RECONCILED to Him. "God was in Christ, reconciling the world unto himself, not imputing their trespasses unto them" (II Corinthians 5:19). Following this word of RECONCILIATION is the invitation, "Be ye reconciled to God." Whoever receives RECONCILIATION for sin is RECONCILED to God. He knows that all his sins are forgiven.

So perfect is the RECONCILIATION and so really has sin been covered and blotted out, that he who believes in Christ is looked upon, and treated by God, as entirely righteous. The acquittal which he has received from God is so complete that there is nothing, absolutely nothing, to prevent him approaching God with the utmost freedom.

For the enjoyment of this blessedness nothing is necessary, save faith in the blood. The blood alone has done absolutely everything.

The penitent sinner, who turns from his sin to God, needs only faith in that blood. That is, faith in the power of the blood, that it has truly atoned for sin and that it really has atoned for him. Through that faith, he knows that he is fully RECONCILED to God, and that there is now not the least thing to hinder God pouring out on him the fullness of His love, and blessing.

Then through the LIVING CHRIST, the powerful effects which the blood has exercised in heaven will increasingly be manifested in your hearts, and you will know what it means to walk, by the Spirit's grace, in the full light and enjoyment of forgiveness.

And to you who have not yet obtained forgiveness of your sins, does not this word come to you as an urgent call to faith in His blood?

The Scarlet Thread

Will you never allow yourselves to be moved by what God has done for you as sinners? "Herein is love, not that we loved God but that he loved us and sent his Son to be the reconciliation for our sins" (I John 4:10).

The precious blood, divine, has been shed, RECONCILIATION is complete, and the message comes to you, "Be ye reconciled to God."

We are told in God's Word that if you repent of your sins, and desire to be delivered from sin's power and bondage, you should exercise faith in the blood. Open your heart to the influence of the word that God has sent to be spoken unto you. Open your heart to the message, that the blood can deliver you, yes, even you, this moment. Only believe it. Say "that blood is also for me." If you come as a guilty, lost sinner, longing for pardon, you may rest assured that the blood which has already made a perfect RECONCILIATION covers your sin and restores you, immediately, to the favor and love of GOD.

So I pray you, exercise faith in the blood. This moment bow down before God, and tell Him that you do believe in the power of the blood for your own soul. Having said that, stand by it, and cling to it. Through faith in His blood, Jesus Christ will be the RECONCILIATION for your sins also.

Chapter Three

SELAH!
THINK ON THESE THINGS

What are the three effects of sin upon?

1. _____
2. _____
3. _____

What does the word "reconciliation" mean?

"_____ _____."

Reconciliation for sin can take place only by _____ and satisfaction is reconciliation.

      Through the LIVING CHRIST, the powerful effects which the blood has exercised in heaven will increasingly be manifested in your hearts and you will know what it means to walk, by the Spirit's grace, in the full light and enjoyment of forgiveness.

      Why not stop for a moment and that Jesus that you have that full light of forgiveness. If you do not have this assurance, why not stop and ask Him now to give you this wonderful truth.

The Scarlet Thread

Yes, dear Christian,

begin to rejoice every day

that your sins are "covered"

by the Blood of the Lamb!

CHAPTER FOUR

Cleansing Through The Blood

I John 1:7

The Scarlet Thread

We have already seen that the most important effect of the Blood is RECONCILIATION for sin.

The fruit of knowledge about, and faith in RECONCILIATION, is the PARDON of sin. Pardon is just a declaration of what has already taken place in heaven on the sinner's behalf, and his hearty acceptance of it.

This first effect of the Blood is not the only one. In proportion as the soul, through faith, yields itself to the Spirit of God to understand and enjoy the full power of RECONCILIATION, the Blood exerts a further power, in the imparting of the other blessings which, in Scripture, are attributed to it.

One of the first results of RECONCILIATION is CLEANSING FROM SIN.

In this chapter we will see what God's Word has to say about this. CLEANSING is often spoken about, among us, as if it were no more than the

Chapter Four

pardon of sins, or the cleansing from guilt. This, however, is not so. Scripture does not speak of being CLEANSED FROM GUILT. One must realize that CLEANSING from sin means deliverance from the pollution, not from the guilt of sin. The guilt of sin concerns our relationship to God. The pollution of sin, on the other hand, is the sense of defilement and impurity, which sin brings to our inner being, and it is with this that CLEANSING has to do.

It is of the greatest importance for every believer who desires to enjoy the full salvation which God has provided for him, to understand aright what the Scriptures teach about this CLEANSING.

O.K. Let's begin on this wonderful lesson.

One of the first results of RECONCILIATION is CLEANSING FROM SIN.

I. WHAT THE WORD CLEANSING MEANS IN THE OLD TESTAMENT.

In the service of God as ordained by the hand of Moses for Israel, there were two ceremonies to be observed by God's people in preparation for approach to Him. These were the OFFERINGS or SACRIFICES and the CLEANSINGS or PURIFICATIONS.

➤ Both were to be observed but in different manners.

The Scarlet Thread

- ➢ Both were intended to remind man how sinful he was, and how unfit to draw near to a holy God.

- ➢ Both were to typify the REDEMPTION by which the Lord Jesus Christ would restore to man fellowship with God. As a rule it is only the OFFERINGS which are regarded as typical of REDEMPTION through Christ. The Epistle to the Hebrews, however, emphatically mentions THE CLEANSINGS as figures "for the time being in which were offered SACRIFICES and DIVERS WASHINGS" (Hebrews 9: 9-10).

If we can imagine the life of an Israelite we would understand that the consciousness of sin, and the need for REDEMPTION, was awakened not less by the CLEANSINGS than the OFFERINGS. We must also learn from them what the power of the Blood of Jesus actually is.

We may take one of the more important cases of CLEANSING as an illustration. In Numbers chapter nineteen, beginning in verse eleven, we find that if anyone was in a hut or house where a dead body lay or if he had even touched a dead body or bones; he was unclean for seven days. Death, as the punishment for sin, made everyone who came into association with it unclean. CLEANSING was accomplished by using the ashes of a young heifer which had been burned, as described in Numbers 19 (Compare Hebrews.9:13, 14). These ashes, mixed with water, were sprinkled by means of a bunch of hyssop on the one who was unclean; he had then to bathe himself in water, after which he was once more ceremonially clean.

The words "UNCLEAN," "CLEANSING," "CLEAN," were used in reference to the healing of leprosy, a disease which might be described as a living death as we find given to us in Leviticus 13-14.

Chapter Four

Here also he who was to be CLEANSED must bathe in water, having been first sprinkled with water, in which the blood of a bird, sacrificially offered, had been mixed. Seven days later he was again sprinkled with sacrificial blood.

As we look at the laws of CLEANSING, they will teach us that the difference between THE CLEANSINGS and THE OFFERINGS was twofold.

- **First:** *The OFFERING* had definite reference to the transgression for which RECONCILIATION had to be made. CLEANSING had more to do with conditions which were not sinful in themselves, but were the result of sin, and therefore must be acknowledged by God's holy people as defiled.

- **Secondly:** *In the case of the OFFERING*, nothing was done to the offering of himself. He saw the blood sprinkled on the altar or carried into the Holy Place; he must believe that this achieved RECONCILIATION before God, but nothing was done to himself. In CLEANSING, on the other hand, what happened to the person was the chief thing. Defilement was something that either through internal disease, or outward touch, had come upon the man; so the washing or sprinkling with water must take place on himself as ordained by God.

CLEANSING was something that he could feel and experience. It brought about a change not only in his relationship to God, but in his own condition. In the OFFERING something was done FOR him; by

CLEANSING, something was done IN him. The OFFERING had respect to his guilt, the CLEANSING to the pollution of sin.

The same meaning of the words "CLEAN," "CLEANSING," is found elsewhere in the Old Testament. David prays in Psalm 51:2, as a result of what took place in II Samuel, chapters one and two. "CLEANSE me from my sin," "Purge me with hyssop and I shall be CLEAN." The word used by David here is that which is used most frequently for the CLEANSING of anyone who had touched a dead body. Hyssop also was used in such cases. David prayed for more than pardon. He confessed that he had been "shapen in iniquity," that his nature was sinful. He prayed that he might be made pure within. "CLEANSE me from my sin," was his prayer. He uses the same word later on when he prays, "Create in me a CLEAN heart, O God." CLEANSING is more than pardon.

CLEANSING by water, by blood, by fire; all of these are typical of the CLEANSING which would take place under the New Covenant, an inner CLEANSING and deliverance from the stain of sin.

II. **THE BLESSING IN THE NEW TESTAMENT BY CLEANSING.**

We often find reference made in the New Testament of a clean or pure heart. Our Lord said, "Blessed are the PURE in heart" (Matthew 5:8); Paul speaks of "love out of a PURE heart" (I Timothy 1:5). Peter encouraged his readers to "love one another with a PURE heart fervently." The word CLEANSING is also used. As regards to ourselves we read, "Let us CLEANSE ourselves from all filthiness of the flesh and spirit" (II Corinthians 7:1).

These and other verses teach us that CLEANSING is an inward word wrought in the heart, and that it is subsequent to pardon.

Chapter Four

We are told in I John 1:7 that, "the blood of Jesus Christ his Son CLEANSETH us from all sin." This word CLEANSETH does not refer to the grace of PARDON received at conversion, but to the effect of grace IN God's children who walk in the light. We read, "If we walk in the light as he is in the light . . . the blood of Jesus Christ his Son CLEANSETH us from all sin." This refers to something more than pardon as it appears from what follows in verse nine, "He is faithful and just to forgive us our sins and to CLEANSE us from all unrighteousness." Cleansing is something that comes after pardon and is the result of it, by the inward and experimental reception of the power of the blood of Jesus in the heart of the believer.

This takes place according to the Word, first in the purifying of the conscience. "How much more shall the blood of Christ PURGE your conscience from dead works to serve the living God" (Hebrews 9:14). The mention already made of the ashes of an heifer sprinkling the unclean typifies a personal experience of the precious blood of Christ. Conscience is not only a judge to give sentence on our actions; it is also the inward voice which bears witness to our relationship to God, and to God's relationship to us! When it is CLEANSED by the blood then it bears witness that we are well pleasing to God. The conscience is CLEANSED - there is no need for the least shadow of separation between God and us; we look up to Him in the full power of REDEMPTION. The conscience CLEANSED by the blood bears witness to nothing less than a complete redemption, the fullness of God's good-pleasure.

And if the conscience is CLEANSED so also is the HEART, of which the conscience is the center. We read of having the heart CLEANSED from an evil conscience (Hebrews 10:22).

Not only must the conscience be CLEANSED but the heart also must be CLEANSED, including the understanding, and the will, with all our thoughts and desires. Through the blood, by the shedding of which Christ delivered Himself up to death, and by virtue of which He entered again into heaven, the death and resurrection of Christ are ceaselessly effectual. By this power of His death and resurrection, sinful lusts, and dispositions, are slain.

"The blood of Jesus Christ cleanseth from all sin," from original, as well as from actual sin. The blood exercises its spiritual, heavenly power in the soul. The believer in whose life the blood is fully efficacious, experiences that the old nature is hindered from manifesting its power. Through the blood, its lusts and desires are subdued and slain, and everything is so CLEANSED that the Spirit can bring forth His glorious fruit.

We have noted a difference between the guilt and the pollution of sin. This is of importance for a clear understanding of the matter; but in actual life we must ever remember that they are not divided. God, through the blood, deals with sin as a whole; every true operation of the blood manifests its power simultaneously over the guilt and the pollution of sin. Reconciliation and cleansing always go together, and the blood is ceaselessly operative.

So then we have found that: In the Old Testament, CLEANSING was necessary for each sin. In the New Testament CLEANSING depends on Christ who ever lives to intercede. When our faith sees and desires and lays hold of this fact, the heart can abide every moment under the protecting and CLEANSING power of the blood.

III. **HOW MAY WE EXPERIENCE THE FULL ENJOYMENT OF THIS BLESSING?**

Everyone who through faith obtains a share in the atoning merit of the blood of Christ has a share also in its CLEANSING power. It is, therefore, of

Chapter Four

great importance to understand what the conditions are for the full enjoyment of this glorious blessing.

> ➢ **KNOWLEDGE IS NECESSARY.**

Many think that pardon of sin is all that we receive through the blood. They ask for and so obtain nothing more.

It is a wonderful thing to begin to see that the Holy Spirit of God has a special purpose in making use of different words in Scripture concerning the effects of the blood. Then we begin to inquire about their special meaning. Every Christian who truly longs to know what the Lord desires to teach us by this one word CLEANSING, will attentively compare all the places in Scripture where the word is used. When we see where CLEANSING is spoken of, we will soon feel that there is more promised to the believer than the removal of guilt. We will begin to understand that CLEANSING through washing can take away stain, and although we cannot fully explain in what way this takes place, we will, however, be convinced that we may expect a blessed inward operation of the CLEANSING away of the effects of sin, by the blood. Knowledge of this truth is the first condition of experiencing it.

> ➢ **THERE MUST BE DESIRE.**

It is to be feared that our Christianity is only too pleased to postpone to a future life the experience of the Beatitude which our Lord intended for our earthly life, "Blessed are the pure in heart, for they shall see God."

It is not regularly preached from many pulpits today that PURITY OF HEART is a characteristic of every child of God, because it is the necessary condition of fellowship with Him, of the enjoyment of His salvation. There is too little inner longing to be really in all things, at all times, well pleasing to the Lord. WHY? Sin and the stain of sin have troubled us too little! With this truth in mind, we need to remember:

- God's Word comes to us with the promise of blessing which ought to awaken all our desires.

- Believe that the blood of Jesus cleanses from all sin. If you learn how to yield yourself to its operation, it can do great things in you.

- Should you not every hour desire to experience the glorious cleansing power to be preserved, in spite of your depraved nature, from the many stains for which your conscience is constantly accusing you?

The desire of every born again believer should be awakened to long for this blessing. Put God to the test to work out in you what He, as the Faithful One, has promised - CLEANSING from all unrighteousness.

➢ **THE THIRD CONDITION IS A WILLINGNESS TO SEPARATE YOURSELF FROM EVERYTHING THAT IS UNCLEAN.**

Because of sin everything in our nature, and in the world, is defiled. CLEANSING cannot take place where there is not an entire separation from it and giving up of everything that is unclean. Paul said in II Corinthians 6:17, "Touch not the unclean thing" is God's command to every believer and few must recognize that all the things surrounding them are unclean.

Oh, dear Christian, our possessions, our spirit, must all be surrendered, that we may be CLEANSED in every relationship by the precious

Chapter Four

blood, and that all the activities of my spirit, soul, and being, may experience a thorough CLEANSING.

Anyone who will keep back anything, however small, cannot obtain the full blessing. He who is willing to pay the full price so as to have his whole being baptized by the blood is on the way to understand fully this word, "the blood of Jesus cleanseth from all sin."

> ➤ **THE LAST CONDITION IS EXERCISING FAITH IN THE POWER OF THE BLOOD.**

It is not as if we, through our faith, bestow its efficacy upon the blood. No, the blood ever retains its power and effectiveness, but our unbelief closes our hearts, and hinders its operation. Faith is simply the removal of that hindrance, the setting open of our hearts, for the divine power by which the living Lord will bestow His blood.

The Scarlet Thread

SELAH!
THINK ON THESE THINGS

"Everyone who through faith obtains a share in the atoning merit of the blood of Christ has a share also in its CLEANSING power. It is, therefore, of great importance to understand what the conditions are for the full enjoyment of this glorious blessing." Can you name these four?

1. _____
2. _____
3. _____
4. _____

Personal notes on this chapter to remember:

_____
_____
_____
_____
_____

Chapter Four

One of the first results of

RECONCILIATION is

CLEANSING FROM SIN.

CHAPTER FIVE

Sanctification Through The Blood

Hebrews 13:12

Chapter Five

_ _ _ _ _ _ _ _ _ _ _ _ _ _ _ _

The subject of our last chapter was "Cleansing through the blood" and now we turn our attention to, **SANCTIFICATION THROUGH THE BLOOD.**

To an unknowing observer, it might seem that there is little difference between CLEANSING and SANCTIFICATION that the two words mean about the same thing; but we must realize the difference is great and important.

CLEANSING has to do chiefly with the old life, and the stain of sin which must be removed, and is only preparatory.

SANCTIFICATION concerns the new life, and that characteristic of it which must be imparted to it by God. SANCTIFICATION, which means union with God, is the peculiar fullness of blessing purchased for us by the blood.

The Scarlet Thread

The distinction between these two things is clearly marked in Scripture. Paul reminds us that, "Christ gave himself for the church, that he might sanctify it, having cleansed it." So then, having first CLEANSED it, then He SANCTIFIES it. Writing to Timothy Paul says, "If a man therefore purge himself from these, he shall be a vessel unto honour, sanctified, and meet for the master's use" (II Timothy 2: 21). SANCTIFICATION is a blessing which follows after, and stronger than CLEANSING.

This is illustrated by the ordinances connected with the consecration of the Priests, compared with that of the Levites. In the case of the latter, who took a lower position than the Priests in the service of the Sanctuary, no mention is made of SANCTIFICATION; but the word CLEANSING is used five times in Numbers chapter 8.

In the consecration of the Priests the word "to SANCTIFY" is often used; for the Priests stood in a closer relationship to God than the Levites as we find in Exodus chapter 19 and in Leviticus chapter 8.

This record at the same time emphasizes the close connection between the sacrificial blood, and SANCTIFICATION. In the case of the consecration of the Levites, RECONCILIATION for sin was made, and they were sprinkled with the water of purification for CLEANSING, but notice they were not sprinkled with blood. But in the consecration of the Priests, blood had to be sprinkled upon them. They were SANCTIFIED by a more personal and intimate application of the blood.

All this was typical of SANCTIFICATION through the BLOOD OF JESUS, and this is what we now seek to understand, that we may obtain a share in it. With this as our introduction to this chapter, let's look at:

Chapter Five

I. WHAT IS SANCTIFICATION?

To better understand what the SANCTIFICATION of the redeemed is, we must first learn what the holiness of God is. He alone is the HOLY ONE. Holiness in the creature must be received from Him.

God's holiness is often spoken of as though it consisted in His hatred of, and hostility to sin; but this gives no explanation of what holiness actually is. It is merely a negative statement that God's holiness cannot bear sin.

Holiness is that attribute of God because of which He always is, and wills, and does what is supremely good; because of which also He desires what is supremely good in His creatures, and bestows it upon them.

God is called "The Holy One" in Scripture, not only because He punishes sin, but also because He is the Redeemer of His people. It is His holiness, which ever wills what is good for all, that moved Him to redeem sinners. Both the WRATH of God which punishes sin, and LOVE of God which redeems the sinner, spring from the same source-His holiness. Holiness is the perfection of God's nature.

Holiness in man is a disposition in entire agreement with that of God; which chooses in all things to will as God wills: as it is written, "As he is holy, so be ye holy" (I Peter 1:15).

Holiness in us is nothing else than oneness with God. The sanctification of God's people is effected by the communication to them of the holiness of God. There is no other way of obtaining SANCTIFICATION, except by God bestowing what He alone possesses. He alone is the HOLY ONE. He is the Lord who sanctifies.

The Scarlet Thread

By the different meanings which Scripture attaches to the words "sanctification" and "to sanctify," a certain relationship with God, into which we are brought, needs to be pointed out.

The first and simplest meaning of the word SANCTIFICATION is "separation." That which is taken out of its surroundings, by God's command, and is set aside or separated as His own possession and for his service - that is holy. This does not mean separation from sin only, but from all that is in the world, even from what may be permissible. Thus God sanctified the seventh day. The other days were not unclean, for God saw all that He had made and "beheld it was very good." But that day alone was holy, which God had taken possession of by His own special act. In the same way God had separated Israel from other nations, and in Israel, had separated the priests, to be holy unto Him. This separation unto SANCTIFICATION is always God's own work, and so the electing grace of God is often closely connected with SANCTIFICATION. "Ye shall be holy unto me . . . I have separated you . . . that ye should be mine" (Leviticus 20:26). "The man whom the Lord shall choose shall be holy" (Numbers 16:7). "Thou art an holy people unto the Lord, the Lord thy God hath chosen thee" (Deuteronomy 7:6). God cannot take part with other lords. He must be the sole possessor, and ruler, of those to whom He reveals and imparts His holiness.

But this separation is not all that is included in the word SANCTIFICATION. It is only the indispensable condition of what must follow. When separated, man stands before God in no respect differing from an object without life that has been sanctified to the service of God. If the separation is to be of value, something more must take place. Man must surrender himself willingly, and heartily, to this separation. SANCTIFICATION includes personal consecration to the Lord to be His.

Chapter Five

SANCTIFICATION can become ours only when it sends down its roots into, and takes up its abode in the depths of our daily personal life; in our will, and in our love.

God sanctifies no man against his will, therefore, the personal, hearty, surrender to God is an indispensable part of SANCTIFICATION.

It is for this reason that the Scriptures not only speak of God sanctifying us, but they say often, that we must sanctify ourselves. But even by consecration, true SANCTIFICATION is not yet complete. Separation and consecration are together only the preparation for the glorious work that God will do, as He imparts His own holiness to the soul. "PARTAKING OF THE DIVINE NATURE" is the blessing which is promised to believers in SANCTIFICATION. "That we might be partakers of his holiness" (Hebrews 12:10), that is the glorious aim of God's work in those whom He separates for Himself.

As God dwelt among the people of Israel to sanctify his people (Exodus 29:45-46), and He dwells in us. It is the presence of God alone that can sanctify. But so surely is this our portion that Scripture does not shrink from speaking of God dwelling in our hearts in such power that we may be "filled unto all the fullness of God." True SANCTIFICATION is fellowship with God and His dwelling in us.

II. THIS SANCTIFICATION WAS THE OBJECT FOR WHICH CHRIST SUFFERED.

This is plainly stated in Hebrews 13:12: "Jesus suffered that he might sanctify his people." In the wisdom of God, a participation in His holiness is the highest destiny of man. Therefore, this was the central object of the coming of our Lord Jesus to earth; and above all, of His sufferings and death. It was "that he might sanctify his people" and "that they might be holy and without blame" (Ephesians 1: 4).

How the sufferings of Christ attained this end, and became our SANCTIFICATION, is made plain to us by the words which He spoke to His Father, when He was about to allow Himself to be bound as a sacrifice. "For their sakes I sanctify myself, that they also may be sanctified through the truth" (John 17: 19).

It is important that we understand that because His sufferings and death were a SANCTIFICATION of Himself that they can become SANCTIFICATION for us.

What does that mean? Simply that Jesus was the HOLY ONE OF GOD, "The Son whom the Father had sanctified and sent into the world," and must He sanctify Himself? He must do so; it was indispensable.

Now watch this statement very closely:

The SANCTIFICATION which He possessed was not beyond the reach of temptation. In His temptation He must maintain it, and show how perfectly His will was surrendered to the holiness of God.

We have seen that true holiness in man is the perfect oneness of His will with that of God. Through all our Lord's life, from the temptation in the wilderness onwards, He had subjected His will to the will of His Father, and had consecrated Himself as a sacrifice to God, but it was chiefly in Gethsemane He did this. There was the hour, and the power of darkness; the temptation to put away the terrible cup of wrath from His lips and to do His own will came with almost irresistible power, but:

- ➢ He rejected the temptation.

Chapter Five

- He offered up Himself, and His will, to the will and holiness of God.

- He sanctified Himself, by a perfect oneness of will, with that of God. This sanctification of Himself has become the power by which we also may be sanctified through the truth.

- This is in perfect accord with what we learn from the Epistle to the Hebrews, where, speaking of the words used by Christ, we read, "I come to do thy will, O God," and then it is added, "By the which will we are sanctified through the offering of the body of Jesus Christ once for all" (Hebrews 10:9-10).

- It was because the offering of His body was His surrender of Himself to do the will of God, that we become sanctified by that will. He sanctified Himself there, for us, that we might be sanctified through the truth.

- It was perfect obedience in which He surrendered Himself, that God's holy will might be accomplished in Him and it was not only the meritorious cause of our salvation, but is at the same time the power by which sin was forever conquered, and by which the same disposition, and the same sanctification, may be created in our hearts.

We also find in Hebrews, the true relationship of our Lord to His own people where it is even more clearly characterized as having SANCTIFICATION for its chief end after, speaking of how becoming it was, that our Lord should suffer as He did, we read, "For both he that sanctifieth and they who are sanctified are all of one" (Hebrews 2: 11). The unity between the Lord Jesus and His people consists in the fact, that they both receive their life from one Father, and both have a share in one and the same

The Scarlet Thread

SANCTIFICATION. Jesus is the sanctifier and we that are saved become the sanctified. SANCTIFICATION is the bond that unites us. "Therefore Jesus also suffered that he might sanctify his people with his own blood."

If we are willing to really understand, and experience what SANCTIFICATION by **THE BLOOD** means, then it is important for us, to first lay fast hold of the fact that SANCTIFICATION is the characteristic, and purpose of all the entire sufferings of our Lord, of which sufferings the blood was the fruit, and means of blessing. His SANCTIFICATION of Himself has the characteristic of those sufferings. Our SANCTIFICATION is the purpose of His sufferings, and only to attain that purpose do they work out the perfect blessing. In proportion as this is clear to us, we shall move forward into the true meaning and blessing of His sufferings.

It was God foreordained redemption. It was His will to glorify His holiness in victory over sin, by the sanctification of man after His own image. It was with the same object that our Lord Jesus endured, and accomplished His sufferings; we must be consecrated to God. RECONCILIATION, PARDON, and CLEANSING from sin, have all an unspeakable value and we must remember that they all point onwards to SANCTIFICATION.

It is God's will that each one who has been redeemed by the precious blood of Jesus Christ, should know that it is a divine mark, characterizing his entire separation to God; that this blood calls him to an undivided consecration to a life, wholly for God, and that this blood is the promise, and the power of a participation in God's holiness, through which God Himself will make His abiding place in him, and be his God.

Oh, that we might understand, and believe that, "Jesus also suffered, that he might sanctify his people, with his own blood" (Hebrews 13:12).

Chapter Five

III. HOW SANCTIFICATION BY THE BLOOD IS TO BE OBTAINED.

To answer this question, in general, is that everyone who is a partaker of the virtue of the blood is also a partaker of SANCTIFICATION, and is in God's sight a sanctified person.

In proportion as we live in close and abiding contact with the blood, we continue to experience, increasingly the blood and its sanctifying effects; even though we still understand but little of how those effects are produced. It is hard to understand how to lay hold of, or explain everything, before we may, by faith, pray that the blood might manifest its sanctifying power in Him. No, it was just in connection with the bath of cleansing, the washing of the disciples' feet that the Lord Jesus said, "What I do thou knowest not now, but thou shalt know hereafter." It is the Lord Jesus Himself who sanctifies His people *"by His own blood."*

Now then, the believer ought to grow in knowledge also; thus only can he enter into the full blessing which is prepared for him. We have not only the right, but it is our duty to inquire earnestly what the essential connection is between the blessed effect of the blood, and our SANCTIFICATION, and in what way the Lord Jesus will work out in us, by His blood, those things which we have ascertained to be the chief qualities of SANCTIFICATION.

Up to this point, we have seen that the beginning of all SANCTIFICATION is SEPARATION to God, as His entire possession and to be at God's disposal. This is just what the blood proclaims, that the power of sin is broken; that we are loosed from its bonds; that we are no longer its bond-servants; but belong to Him who purchased our freedom with His blood?

The Scarlet Thread

"Ye are not your own, ye are bought with a price;" this is the language in which the blood tells us that we are God's possession. Because He desires to have us entirely for Himself, He has chosen and bought us, and set upon us the distinguishing mark of the blood, as those who are separated from all around them, to live only for His service. This idea of separation is clearly expressed in the words we so often repeat, "Jesus that he might sanctify his people with his own blood, suffered without the gate. Let us go forth therefore unto him without the camp bearing his reproach." "Going out" from all that is of this world, was the characteristic of Him who was holy, undefiled, separate from sinners; and it must be the characteristic of all His followers.

As a Christian, the Lord Jesus HAS SANCTIFIED you through His own blood, and He desires to make you experience, through that blood, the full power of this SANCTIFICATION. Why not endeavor to gain a clear impression of what has taken place in you through the sprinkling of that blood. The holy God desires to have you entirely for Himself. The Bible tells us that "you have been bought with a price," so then no one, nothing, may any longer have the least right over you, nor have you any right over yourself. God has separated you unto HIMSELF, and that you might feel this He set His mark upon you. That mark is the most wonderful thing that is to be found on earth or in heaven, **"THE BLOOD OF JESUS."** The blood in which the life of the eternal Son of God is; the blood that on the throne of grace is ever before God's face; the blood that assures you of full redemption from the power of sin; that blood is sprinkled upon you, as a sign that you belong to God.

As a believer, I pray that you let every thought about the blood awaken in you the glorious confession, **"*By his own blood***, the Lord Jesus has sanctified me, He has taken complete possession of me for God, and I belong entirely to God."

Chapter Five

We have seen that SANCTIFICATION is more than separation. That is only the beginning. We have seen also that personal consecration and hearty and willing surrender to live only for, and in God's holy will, is part of SANCTIFICATION.

In what way can the blood of Christ work out this surrender in us, and SANCTIFY in us who have surrendered? The answer is not difficult. It is not enough to believe in the power of the blood to redeem us, and to free us from sin, but we must, above all, notice the source of this power.

We know that it has this power, because of the willingness with which the Lord Jesus surrendered Himself. In the shedding of His blood He sanctifies: Himself, offered Himself entirely to God and His holiness. It is because of this that the blood is so holy, and possesses such sanctifying power and in the blood we have an impressive representation of the self-surrender of Christ. The blood will ever speak of the consecration of Jesus to the Father, as the opening of the way, and supplying the power for victory over sin. And the closer we come into contact with the blood, and the more we live under the deep impression of having been sprinkled by the blood, we shall hear more clearly the voice of the blood declare that, "Total surrender to God" is the way to full redemption from sin.

The voice of the blood will not speak simply to teach us or to awaken thought; the blood speaks with a divine and life giving power. What it commands, that it bestows. It works out in us the same disposition that was in our Lord Jesus. **By His own blood** Jesus sanctifies us that we, holding nothing back, might surrender ourselves with all our hearts to the holy will of God.

The Scarlet Thread

But CONSECRATION itself even along with any following SEPARATION is still only a preparation. Entire Sanctification takes place when God takes possession of and falls with His glory the temple that is consecrated to Him. "There I will meet with the children of Israel, and they shall be sanctified by my glory" (Exodus 29:43). Actual, complete SANCTIFICATION consists in God's impartation of His own holiness of Himself.

Here also the blood speaks. It tells us that heaven is opened, that the powers of the heavenly life have come down to earth, that every hindrance has been removed, and God can make His abode with man.

Immediate nearness and fellowship with God are made possible by the blood. The believer, who surrenders himself unreservedly to the blood, obtains the full assurance that God will bestow Himself wholly, and will reveal His holiness in him.

How glorious are the results of such SANCTIFICATION! Through the Holy Spirit, the soul's intercourse is in the living experience of God's abiding nearness; accompanied by the awakening of the tenderest carefulness against sin; guarded by caution and the fear of God.

But to live in watchfulness against sin does not satisfy the soul. The temple must not only be cleansed, but it must be filled with God's glory. "All the virtues of divine holiness, as manifested in the Lord Jesus, are to be sought for and found, in fellowship with God. Sanctification means union with God; fellowship in His will; sharing His life; conformity to His image."

Christians, "Wherefore Jesus also . . . suffered without the gate that He might sanctify His people with **His own blood**. Let us go forth unto Him without the camp." Yes, it is He who sanctifies His people. "Let us go forth

Chapter Five

unto Him." Let us trust Him to make known to us the power of the blood. Let us yield ourselves wholly to its blessed efficacy. That blood, through which He sanctified Himself, has entered heaven to open it for us. It can make our hearts also a throne of God that the grace and glory of God may dwell in us. Yes; "let us go forth unto him without the camp." He who is willing to lose, and say farewell to everything, in order that Jesus may sanctify him, will not fail to obtain the blessing. He, who is willing at any cost to experience the full power of the precious blood, can confidently reckon that he will be sanctified by Jesus Himself, through that blood.

The Scarlet Thread

SELAH!
THINK ON THESE THINGS

Describe Sanctification-

_____
_____
_____
_____

"Sanctification can become ours only when it sends down its roots into, and takes up its abode in the depths of our daily personal life; in our will, and in our live."

Read Ephesians chapter one and verse four again and rejoice in this wonderful relationship with Christ!

Chapter Five

That mark is the most wonderful thing that is to be found on earth or in heaven,

"**THE BLOOD OF JESUS**."

CHAPTER SIX

There is Life in The Blood

John 6:53-56

Chapter Six

The crucifixion of Jesus is an essential element in producing saving faith. It is not only that Jesus died for sinners, as such, but the dying of Jesus Christ fixed a pattern and a procedure for believers to follow. The Christian must partake of the death of Christ and he must be crucified with Him. Paul knew this from his own experience:

"I am crucified with Christ: nevertheless I live; yet not I, but Christ liveth in me: and the life which I now live in the flesh I live by the faith of the Son of God, who loved me, and gave himself for me" (Galatians 2:20).

In teaching this truth Paul later discussed, Jesus used a very simple figure of speech - the eating of His flesh and the drinking of His blood. His hearers stumbled over this, as men and women have been stumbling over it ever since. The human heart draws back from the need of self-denial. It is very significant that Jesus set forth no argument. He used no further words to explain what He meant. He simply set forth this truth, and challenged them to accept or reject it. He made it unmistakably plain to all that salvation was available only to those who would join Him in His death.

Difficult as this language first appears, it is really blessedly simple. It is not a dead Christ which the sinner is to feed upon, but on the death of One who is now alive forever more. His death is mine, when appropriated by faith; and thus appropriated, it becomes life in me. The figure of "eating" looks back, perhaps, to Genesis 3. Man died, spiritually, by "eating" of the forbidden fruit and he is made alive spiritually by an act of eating!

"Whoso eateth my flesh, and drinketh my blood, hath eternal life; and I will raise him up at the last day" (John 6:54). Notice the change in the tense of the verb. In the previous verse it is, "Except ye eat;" here it is "whoso eateth." In the former, the verb is in the aorist tense, implying a single act, an act done once for all. In the latter, the verb is in the perfect tense, denoting that which is continuous and characteristic. Verse 53 defines the difference between one who is lost and one who is saved. In order to be saved, I must "eat" the flesh and "drink" the blood of the Son of man; that is, I must appropriate Him, make Him mine by an act of faith.

This act of receiving Christ is done once for all. I cannot receive Him a second time, for He never leaves me! But, having received Him to the saving of my soul, I now feed on Him constantly, daily, as the Food of my soul. Exodus 12 supplies us with an illustration. First, the Israelite was to apply the shed blood of the slain lamb. Then, as protected by that blood, he was to feed on the lamb itself.

"Whoso eateth my flesh, and drinketh my blood, hath eternal life; and I will raise him up at the last day." This confirms our interpretation of the previous verse. If we compare it with verse 47, it will be seen at once the "eating" is equivalent to "believing." Note, too, that the tense of the verbs is the same: verse 47 "believeth," verse 54 "eateth." And observe how each of these are evidences of eternal

Chapter Six

life, already in possession of the one thus engaged: "He that believeth on me hath eternal life;" "Whoso eateth my flesh, and drinketh my blood, hath eternal life."

This passage in John 6 is a favorite one with Ritualists, who understand it to refer to the Lord's Supper. But this is certainly a mistake and that for the following reasons:

First, the Lord's Supper had not been instituted when Christ delivered this discourse.

Second, Christ was here addressing Himself to unbelievers, and the Lord's Supper is for saints, not unregenerate sinners.

Third, the eating and drinking here spoken of are in order to salvation; but eating and drinking at the Lord's Table are for those who have been saved.

"For my flesh is meat indeed, and my blood is drink indeed" (John 6:55). The connection between this and the previous verse is obvious. It is brought in, no doubt, to prevent a false inference being drawn from the preceding words. Christ had thrown the emphasis on the "eating." Except a man ate His flesh, he had no life in him.

But now our Lord brings out the truth that there is nothing meritorious in the act of eating; that is to say, there is no mystical power in eating, itself. The nourishing power is in the food eaten; and the potency of faith lies in its Object.

"For my flesh is meat indeed, and my blood is drink indeed." Here Christ throws the emphasis on what it is which must be "eaten." It is true in the natural realm. It is not the mere eating of anything which will nourish us. If a man eats anything that is poisonous, he will die; if he eat that which is not nutritious, he will starve. Equally so is it spiritually. "There are many in hell and on the road to hell; WHY? They believed a lie, and not the truth as it is in Christ Jesus." It is Christ who alone can save: Christ as crucified, but now alive for evermore.

"He that eateth my flesh, and drinketh my blood, dwelleth in me, and I in him" (John 6:56). In this, and the following verse, Christ proceeds to state some of the blessed effects of eating.

It is that the saved sinner is brought into vital union with Christ, and enjoys the most intimate fellowship with Him. The word "dwelleth" is commonly translated "abideth." It always has reference to communion. But mark the tense of the verb: it is only the one who "eateth" and "drinketh" constantly that abides in unbroken fellowship with Christ.

"He that eateth my flesh, and drinketh my blood, dwelleth in me, and I in him." This language clearly implies, though it does not specifically mention the fact that Christ would rise from the dead, for only as risen could He dwell in the believer, and the believer in Him. It is, then, with Christ raised, that they who feed on Him as slain, are identified - so marvelously identified, that Scripture here, for the first time, speaks of union with our blessed Lord. NOW THEN: follow me a little more in this thought; when water is used for washing it cleanses, but if we drink it we are refreshed and revived. He who desires to know the full power of the blood of Jesus must be taught by Him what the blessing of drinking the blood is. Everyone knows the difference there is between washing and drinking. Necessary and pleasant as it is to use water for cleansing, it is much more necessary and reviving to drink it. Without its cleansing it is not possible to live as we ought; but without drinking we cannot live at all. It is only by drinking that we enjoy the full benefit of its power to sustain life.

Chapter Six

Without drinking the blood of the Son of God -- is without the heartiest appropriation of it -- life cannot be obtained.

To many there is something unpleasant in the phrase "drinking the blood of the Son of man," but it was still more disagreeable to the Jews, for the use of blood was forbidden by the law of Moses, under severe penalties (Genesis 9:4). When Jesus spoke of "drinking his blood," it naturally annoyed them-but it was an unspeakable offence to their religious feelings. Our Lord, we may be sure, would not have used the phrase, had He been able otherwise to make plain to them, and to us, the deepest and most glorious truths concerning salvation by the blood.

In this chapter I hope to help you better understand this with three thoughts.

I. **WHAT THE BLESSING IS WHICH IS DESCRIBED AS "DRINKING THE BLOOD."**

We have seen that drinking expresses a much more intimate connection with water than washing, and thereby produces a more powerful effect. There is a blessing in the fellowship with the blood of Jesus which goes much farther than CLEANSING, or SANCTIFICATION; or rather we are enabled to see how far reaching is the influence of the blessing indicated by this phrase.

Not only must the blood do something FOR us, by placing us in a new relationship to God; but it must do something IN us, entirely renewing us within. It is to this that the words of the Lord Jesus draw our attention when He says: "Unless ye eat the flesh of the Son of man, and drink his blood, ye have no life in you." Our Lord distinguishes two kinds of life. The Jews, there, in His presence, had a natural life of body and soul. Many among them were devout, well intentioned men, but He said they had no life in them unless they "ate his flesh and drank his blood." They needed another life, a new heavenly life, which He possessed and which He could impart.

 NOT ONLY MUST THE BLOOD DO SOMETHING *FOR* US,

BY PLACING US IN A NEW RELATIONSHIP TO GOD;

BUT IT MUST DO SOMETHING *IN* US,

ENTIRELY RENEWING US WITHIN.

Every life must obtain nourishment outside of itself. The natural life was naturally nourished, by bread and water. The heavenly life must be nourished by heavenly food and drink, by Jesus Himself. "Except ye eat the flesh of the Son of man, and drink his blood, ye have no life in you." Nothing less must become ours than His life, the life that He, as Son of man, lived on earth.

Our Lord emphasized this still more strongly in words which follow, in which He again explained what the nature of that life is: "Whoso eateth my flesh and DRINKETH MY BLOOD hath eternal life and I will raise him up at the last day."

- Eternal life is the life of God. Our Lord came to earth, in the first place, to reveal that eternal life and the flesh and then to communicate it to us who are in the flesh. In Him we see the eternal life dwelling in its divine power, in a body of flesh; which was taken up into heaven.

Chapter Six

- He tells us that those who eat His flesh and drink His blood, who partake of His body as their sustenance, will experience also in their own bodies the power of eternal life. "I will raise him up at the last day."

- The marvel of the eternal life in Christ is that it was eternal life in a human body. We must be partakers of that body, not less than in the activities of His Spirit, and then our body, also, possessing that life, will one day be raised from the dead.

Our Lord said: "My flesh is meat indeed and **MY BLOOD** is drink indeed." The word translated "indeed" here is the same as that He used when He spoke His parable of the True Vine, "I am the true [the indeed] vine," thus indicating the difference between what was only a symbol and what is actual truth. Earthly food is no REAL food, for it imparts no real life. The one true food is the body and blood of the Lord Jesus Christ which imparts and sustains life. It is not to be used as a shadowy or merely a symbolical manner. No, this word so frequently repeated, indicates that in a full and real sense the flesh and blood of the Lord Jesus are the food by which eternal life is nourished and sustained in us, "My flesh is meat INDEED, and my blood is drink INDEED."

In order to point out the reality and power of this food our Lord added: "He that eateth my flesh and drinketh *my blood* dwelleth in me and I in him." Nourishment by His flesh and blood affects the most perfect union with Him.

This is the reason that His flesh and blood has such power of eternal life. Our Lord declares here, that those who believe in Him are to experience not only certain influences from Him in their hearts, but we are brought into the most close and abiding union with Him. *"HE that DRINKETH MY BLOOD DWELLETH IN ME AND I IN HIM."*

The Scarlet Thread

This then is the blessing of drinking the blood of the Son of man, becoming one with Him, becoming a partaker of the divine nature in Him. How real this union is may be seen from the words which follow: "As I live by the Father, so he that eateth me even he shall live by me." Nothing, save the union which exists between our Lord and the Father, can serve as a type of our union with Him. Just as in the invisible, divine nature, the two Persons are truly one, so man becomes one with Jesus; the union is just as real as that in the divine nature, only with this difference, that as human nature cannot exist apart from the body, this union includes the body also.

II. **HOW THIS BLESSING IS SHAPED IN US: or what the** *"drinking of the blood of Jesus"* **really is.**

The idea here presents itself is that "drinking" indicates the deep, true appropriation in our spirit, by faith, of all we understand concerning the power of the blood.

We speak sometimes of "drinking in" the words of a speaker, when we heartily give ourselves up to listen and receive them. So when the heart of anyone is filled with a sense of the preciousness and power of the blood; when he, with real joy, is lost in the contemplation of it; when he, with wholehearted faith, takes it for himself, and seeks to be convinced in his inner being of the life-giving power of that blood; then it may be rightly said that he *"drinks the blood of Jesus."* All that faith enables him to see of REDEMPTION, of CLEANSING, of SANCTIFICATION by the blood, he absorbs into the depths of his soul.

There is a deep truth in this representation, and it gives us a very glorious demonstration of the way in which the full blessing by the blood may be obtained. And yet it is certain that our Lord intended something more than

Chapter Six

this by so repeatedly making use of the expression about "eating his flesh and drinking his blood." What this further truth is becomes clear by his institution of THE LORD'S SUPPER. For, although our Savior did not actually deal with that Supper when He taught in Capernaum, yet He spoke on the subject of which later on The Supper was made the visible confirmation.

All that has been said up to now about the Supper must have its full application to *"The drinking of the blood of Jesus."* It is a deep spiritual mystery in which the most intimate, the most perfect union with Christ, is affected. It takes place where the soul, through the Holy Spirit, fully appropriates the communion of the blood of Christ, and becomes a true partaker of the very disposition which He revealed in the shedding of His blood. The blood is the soul, the life of the body; where the believer as one body with Christ desires to abide perfectly in Him. And through the Spirit, in a superhuman powerful way, the blood will support and strengthen the heavenly life. The life that was poured out, the blood becomes his life. The life of the old "I" dies to make room for the life of Christ in him. By perceiving how this drinking is the highest participation in the heavenly life of the Lord, faith has one of its highest and most glorious offices.

III. WHAT SHOULD BE OUR ATTITUDE TOWARDS THIS BLESSING?

Well now, you have already seen that we have here, what I believe is one of the deepest mysteries of the life of God in us, so it is advantageous for us to draw near with very deep reverence while we ask the Lord Jesus to teach us and bestow upon us what He means by this *"drinking of His blood."*

"He that drinketh *my blood* dwelleth in me and I in him."

➢ Let me say that those who are satisfied with just the forgiveness of his sins; he who does not thirst to be made to drink abundantly of the love of Jesus.

The Scarlet Thread

- ➢ Those who do not desire to experience redemption for soul and body, in its full power, so as to have truly in himself the same disposition that was in Jesus, will have but a small share in this "***drinking of the blood.***"

- ➢ Those who, sets before him as his chief object, that which is also the object of Jesus: "abide in me and I in you;" who desires that the power of eternal life should operate in his body; he will not suffer himself to be frightened by an impression that these words are too high or too mysterious. He longs to become heavenly minded because he belongs to heaven, and is going there;

- ➢ Therefore he desires to obtain his meat and drink also from heaven. Without thirst, there is no drinking. The longing after Jesus and perfect fellowship with Him is the thirst which is the best preparation for being made to drink the blood.

IT IS BY THE HOLY SPIRIT THAT THE THIRSTY SOUL WILL BE MADE TO DRINK OF THE HEAVENLY REFRESHMENT OF THIS LIFE GIVING DRINK.

We have already said that this drinking is a heavenly mystery. In heaven, where God, the judge of all is, and where Jesus the Mediator of the New Covenant is, there also is "the blood of sprinkling" (Hebrews 12: 23-24). When the Holy Spirit teaches us - taking us, as it were, by the hand - He bestows more than our merely human understanding can grasp. All the thoughts that we can entertain

Chapter Six

about the blood or the life of Jesus about our share in that blood, as members of His body; and about the impartation to us of the living power of that blood; all are but feeble rays of the glorious reality, which He, the Holy Spirit, will bring into being in us through our union with Jesus.

So then in our human bodies, do we find that the blood is actually received, and as it were drunk in? Is it not where one member of the body after another, through the veins, receives the blood-stream which is continually renewed from the heart? Each member of a healthy body ceaselessly and abundantly drinks in the blood----So the Spirit of Life in Christ Jesus, who unites us to Him, will make this drinking of the blood the natural action of the inner life. When the Jews complained that what the Lord had spoken concerning eating His flesh and drinking His blood was "a hard saying," (John 6:60); He said "it is the Spirit that quickeneth; the flesh profiteth nothing" (John 6:63). One must understand that it is the Holy Spirit who makes this divine mystery LIFE AND POWER in us; a true living experience, in which we abide in Jesus and He in us.

The wonderful discourse in the synagogue, following the one given to the people on the outside, was now over. We are here shown the effect of it on the disciples. A "disciple" means one who is a learner. These "disciples" are carefully distinguished from "the twelve." They were made up of a class of people who were, in measure, attracted by the person of Christ and who were, more especially, impressed by His miracles. But how real this attraction was, and how deep the impression made, we are now given to see.

- When Christ had presented Himself not as the Wonder-worker, but as the Bread of God;

- When He had spoken of giving His flesh for the life of the world, and of men drinking His blood, which signified that He would die, and die a death of violence;

- When He insisted that except they ate His flesh and drank His blood "they had no life" in them; and, above all;

- When He announced that man is so depraved and so alienated from God, that except the Father draw him, he would never come to Christ for salvation.

They were all offended. It will be seen then, that we take the words; "This is a hard saying; who can hear it?" as referring to the whole of the discourse which Christ had just delivered in the Capernaum synagogue.

Many of his disciples, when they had heard this, said, "this is an hard saying; who can hear it?" The simple meaning of this is that these disciples were offended. It was not that they found the language of Christ so obscure as to be unintelligible, but what they had heard was so irreconcilable with their own views that they would not receive it and what their own views were comes out plainly in John 12. When Christ signified what death He should die, "The people answered him, 'we have heard out of the law that Christ abideth for ever: and how sayest thou, The Son of man must be lifted up?'" (John 12:34).

In applying the above verse to ourselves, two things should be noted:

First, that when today professing Christians criticize a servant of God who is really giving out Divine truth, and complain that his teaching is "An hard saying," it is always to be traced back to the same cause as operated here. Many disciples will still reject the Word of God when it is ministered in the power of the Spirit, and they will do so because

Chapter Six

it conflicts with their own views and contradicts the traditions of their fathers!

Secondly, notice that these men complained among themselves. This is evident from John 6:61: "When Jesus knew in himself that his disciples murmured at it."

They did not come directly to Christ and openly state their difficulties. They did not ask Him to explain His meaning. Why? Because they were not really anxious for truth and revelation.

Had they been so, they would have sought it from Him. Again we say, How like human nature today! When the Lord's messenger delivers a word that is distasteful to his hearers, they are not manly enough to come to him and tell him their grievance, far less will they approach him seeking help. No, like the miserable cowards they are, they will skulk in the background, seeking to sow the seeds of dissension by criticizing what they have heard.

And such people the servant of God will have no difficulty in placing: they may wear the badge of disciples, but he will know from their actions and speech that they are not believers!

"When Jesus knew in himself that his disciples murmured at it, he said unto them, doth this offend you?" (John 6:61). How solemn this is! These men could not deceive Christ even though:

- They might have walked with Him for a time (verse 66); they might have posed as His disciples (verse 60);

- They might have taken their place in the synagogue (verse 59), and listened with seeming attention and reverence while He taught them; but He knew their hearts: those they could not hide from Him. Nor

The Scarlet Thread

can men do so today. He is not misled by all the religiosity of the day. His eyes of fire pierce through every mask of hypocrisy. Learn, then, the consummate folly and utter worthlessness of "a form of godliness" without its power (II Timothy 3:5).

"When Jesus knew in himself that his disciples murmured at it, he said unto them, Doth this offend you?" How this evidenced, once more, His deity! At the beginning of our chapter He had been regarded as a "prophet;" but a greater than a prophet was here. Later, an insulting contrast had been drawn between Moses and Christ; but a greater than Moses was before them. Neither Moses nor any of the prophets had been able to read the hearts of men. But here was One who knew in Himself when these disciples murmured. He knew, too, why they murmured. He knew they were offended. Plainly, then, this must be God Incarnate, for none but the Lord Himself can read the heart.

"It is the Spirit that quickeneth: the flesh profiteth nothing" (John 6:63). This is indeed a searching word and one that greatly needs emphasizing today in our churches and from the pulpits.

The flesh "profiteth nothing." The flesh has no part in the works of God. All fleshly activities amount to nothing where the regeneration of dead sinners is concerned.

We must believe that all the precious blood can do, or bestow, is really for us.

Have you felt the pull of popular opinion? Have you let Satan try to sway you to stay away from church, to neglect prayer, not to open your Bible day by day? If this is true, why not stop for a moment and think: IS THIS REALLY WHAT YOU WANT TO DO? Now is the time for you and me

Chapter Six

to throw ourselves at His feet and give Him our all in all and life and take a stand for God and His Word.

THERE MUST BE

ON OUR PART

A QUIET, STRONG,

SETTLED EXPECTANCY OF FAITH,

THAT THIS BLESSING WILL BE BESTOWED

ON US.

The Scarlet Thread

_ _ _ _ _ _ _ _ _ _ _ _ _ _ _ _ _

SELAH!
THINK ON THESE THINGS

    The dying of Jesus Christ fixed a _____ and a _____ for believers to follow. With this said, what must the Christian do to be crucified with Him? _____ of the _____ of Christ. Can you recall the passage of Scripture that solidifies this statement?

    It is by the Holy Spirit that the _____ _____ will be made to drink of the Heavenly refreshment of this _____ _____ drink.

    When was the last time that you took a stand for the gospel and its message and what was the result?
_____
_____
_____

CHAPTER SEVEN

Victory Through The Blood

Revelation 12:1-12

The Scarlet Thread

*F*or thousands of years there had been a mighty conflict for the possession of mankind.

Often it seemed as though the kingdom of God had come in power; then at other times the might of Satan seemed to be in control. So then by the Lord Jesus' coming, His wonderful words and works, the most glorious expectations of a speedy redemption were awakened. How terrible was the disappointment which the death of Jesus brought to all who had believed in Him and it seemed, indeed, as if the powers of sin and darkness had conquered, and had established them a kingdom forever.

But, "Through death, **JESUS** has destroyed him that had the power of death, that is the devil," and in that holy moment when our Lord shed His blood in death, and it seemed as if Satan were victorious. The adversary was robbed of the authority he had hitherto possessed.

Praise the Lord our text gives a very grand representation of these memorable events. The best commentators, notwithstanding differences in

Chapter Seven

details of exposition, are united in thinking, that we have here a vision of the casting out of Satan from heaven, as a result of the Ascension of Christ.

Then follows the song from which the text is taken: Revelation 12:10 that reads, "And I heard a loud voice saying in heaven, Now is come salvation, and strength, and the kingdom of our God, and the power of his Christ: for the accuser of our brethren is cast down, which accused them before our God day and night."

The point which deserves our special attention is, that while the conquest of Satan, and his being cast out of heaven, is first represented as the result of the Ascension of Jesus and the war in heaven which followed, yet in the song of triumph which was heard in heaven, victory is ascribed chiefly to ***THE BLOOD OF THE LAMB***; this was the power by which the victory was gained.

Through the whole book of the Revelation we see the Lamb on the Throne. It is a fact that the Lamb has gained that position; ***THE VICTORY OVER SATAN AND ALL HIS AUTHORITY IS BY THE BLOOD OF THE LAMB.***

Thus far we have talked about the blood in its many ways, how it affects us, and it is fitting that we should seek to understand how it is that victory is always ascribed to ***THE BLOOD OF THE LAMB***.

In this chapter we look at three victories.

I. THE VICTORY WHICH WAS GAINED ONCE FOR ALL.

In the exalted representation given in our text we see what a high position was once occupied by Satan, the greatest enemy of the human race.

The Scarlet Thread

- ➤ We know how this is taught in the Old Testament. In the book of Job, we see Satan coming, with the Sons of God, to present himself before the Lord; and to obtain permission from Him to tempt His servant Job (Job 2).

- ➤ In the book of Zechariah 3:1-2; we read that he saw "Joshua the High Priest standing before the angel of the Lord, and Satan standing at his right hand to resist him."

- ➤ Then there is the statement of our Lord, recorded in Luke 10: 18, "I beheld Satan as lightning fall from heaven." Later on, in His agony of soul, as He felt beforehand His approaching sufferings, He said, "Now is the judgment of this world, now shall the prince of this world be cast out" (John 12:31).

It may, at first thought, seem strange that the Scriptures should represent Satan as being in heaven; but to understand this correctly, it is necessary to remember that Heaven is not a small, dwelling place, where God and Satan had fellowship as neighbors. Not so, Heaven is an illimitable (bounded) sphere, with very many different divisions, filled with innumerable hosts of angels, who carry out God's will in nature. Among them, Satan held a place. Then remember, he is not represented in Scripture to be the black, grisly figure in outward appearance as he is generally pictured, but as "an angel of light." He was a prince, with ten thousands of servants.

When he had brought about the fall of man, and had also transferred the world to himself and became its prince, he had real authority over all that was in it. Man had been destined to be king of this world, for God has said, "Have thou authority." When Satan had conquered the king, he took his entire kingdom under his authority; and this authority was recognized by God. God,

Chapter Seven

in His holy will, had ordained that if man listened to Satan, he must suffer the consequences, and become subject to his tyranny. God never in this matter used His power or exercised force, but always took the way of Law and Right; and so Satan retained his authority until it was taken from him in a lawful manner.

This is the reason why he could appear before God in heaven, as accuser of the brethren and in opposition to them for the 4,000 years of the Old Covenant.

He had obtained authority over all flesh, and only after he was conquered **IN FLESH, AS THE SPHERE OF HIS AUTHORITY**, could he be cast out for ever, as accuser, from the Court of Heaven.

So then, the Son of God, also, had to come **IN FLESH** in order to fight and conquer Satan, on his own ground.

For this reason also, at the commencement of His public life, our Lord after His anointing, was openly recognized as the Son of God, "was led by the Spirit into the wilderness to be tempted of the devil." Victory over Satan could be gained only after He had personally endured and resisted his temptations.

It was through His death, and the shedding of His blood, that the Lord Jesus fulfilled the law's demands. So then, the law had been declaring that, "The wages of sin is death;" "The soul that sinneth: shall die." When the law had been thus perfectly fulfilled, the authority of sin and Satan was brought to an end. Therefore, death could not hold Him. "Through the blood of the everlasting covenant" God brought Him "again from the dead." We are also told that He "entered heaven by *his own blood*," to make **His RECONCILIATION** effective for us.

The Scarlet Thread

In the book of Daniel, chapters 10 and 12, we read of a previous conflict between this Michael, who stood on the side of God's people Israel; and the opposing world powers. But only now can Satan be cast out because of the blood of the Lamb. Reconciliation for sin and the fulfillment of the law have taken from him (Satan), all his authority, and right. The blood, as we have already seen, that had done such wonderful things in heaven, with God, in blotting out sin, and bringing it to naught, had a similar power over Satan. He has now no longer any right to accuse. "Now is come salvation, and strength, and the kingdom of our God, and the power of his Christ, for the accuser of our brethren is cast down . . . . And they overcame him by the ***blood of the lamb***."

II. THERE IS A PROGRESSIVE VICTORY.

This is indicated in the words of the Song of Victory, "They overcame him ***by the blood of the Lamb***." This was primarily spoken concerning "the brethren" mentioned, but it refers also to the victory of the angels. The victory in heaven and on earth progresses simultaneously, resting on the same ground.

We know from the portion in Daniel already mentioned (Daniel 10:12-13) what fellowship there exists between heaven and earth in carrying on the work of God. As soon as Daniel prayed the angel became active, and the three weeks' strife in the heavenlies, were three weeks of prayer and fasting on earth. The conflict here on earth is the result of a conflict in the invisible region of the heavenlies. Michael and his angels, as well as the brethren on earth, gained the victory "by the blood of the Lamb."

In the twelfth chapter of Revelation we are clearly taught how the conflict was removed from heaven to earth. "Woe to the inhabitants of the earth" exclaimed the voice in heaven, "for the devil is come down unto you, having great wrath, because he knoweth that he hath but a short time." "And when

Chapter Seven

the dragon saw that he was cast down unto the earth, he persecuted the woman which brought forth the man-child."

The woman signifies nothing else than the church of God, out of which Jesus was born: when the devil could not harm Him anymore, what does he do, he persecutes His church.

- ➤ The disciples of our Lord, and the church in the first three centuries had experience of this.

- ➤ In the bloody persecutions in which hundreds of thousands of Christians perished as martyrs, Satan did his utmost to lead the church into apostasy, or to root it out altogether; but in its full sense, the statement that "they overcame *by the blood of the Lamb*, and by the word of their testimony; and they loved not their lives even unto death" applies to the martyrs.

We must remember that since the days of the Reformation it is still apparent that in proportion as *the blood of the Lamb* is gloried in, the church is constantly inspired by a new life to obtain the victory over deadness or error. Yes, even in the midst of the wildest heathen, where the throne of Satan has been undisturbed for thousands of years, this is still the weapon by which its power must be destroyed. The preaching of *"the blood of the cross"* as the **RECONCILIATION** for the sin of the world, and the ground of God's free, forgiving love, is the power by which the most darkened heart is opened and softened, and from being a dwelling place of Satan is changed into a temple of the Most High.

The Scarlet Thread

That which is available for the church, is available also for each Christian. In *"the blood of the Lamb,"* he always has victory. I believe that when the soul lives in the power of the blood, that the temptations of Satan cease to ensnare.

Where the holy *blood of the Lamb* is sprinkled, there God dwells, and Satan is put to flight. In heaven, and on earth, and in our hearts, those words as the announcement of a **PROGRESSIVE VICTORY** is valid, "They overcame him *by the blood of the Lamb.*"

III. **WE ALSO HAVE A SHARE IN THIS VICTORY** if we are reckoned among those who have been cleansed *"in the blood of the Lamb."*

To better understand this we must pay attention to the following facts:

> **THERE CAN BE NO VICTORY WITHOUT CONFLICT.**

We must recognize that we dwell in an enemy's territory. What was revealed to the apostle in his heavenly vision must hold well in our daily lives. Satan has been cast down into the earth, he has great wrath because he has but a short time. He cannot now reach the glorified Jesus, but seeks to reach Him by attacking His people. We must live always under the holy consciousness that we are watched, every moment, by an enemy of unimaginable cunning and power; that is unwearied in his endeavor to bring us entirely or even partially, however little it may be under his authority. He is literally "the prince of this world." All that is in the world is ready to serve him, and he knows how to make use of it in his attempts to lead the church to be unfaithful to her Lord; and to inspire her with his spirit, the spirit of the world.

Chapter Seven

He makes use, not only of temptations to what is commonly esteemed to be sin, but he knows how to gain an entrance into our earthly engagements and businesses; in the seeking for our daily bread and necessary deeds; in our politics; our commercial combinations; our literature and science, yes even in our churches, in our knowledge; and all things, and, so, to make all that is lawful in itself into a tool to forward his devilish deceptions.

- The believer who desires to share in the victory over Satan "*through the blood of the Lamb*" must be a fighter.

- He must take pains to understand the character of his enemy.

- He must allow himself to be taught by the Spirit through the Word what the secret cunning of Satan is, which is called in Scripture.

> ➢ **VICTORY IS THROUGH FAITH.**

We are told in I John 5:4-5, "For whatsoever is born of God overcometh the world: and this is the victory that overcometh the world, even our faith. Who is he that overcometh the world, but he that believeth that Jesus is the Son of God?"

We are told that this faith can inspire courage and joy in the strife. ***JESUS IS THE VICTOR***; so we need only to have our souls filled with the heavenly vision of Satan being cast out of heaven by Jesus; filled with faith in the blood by which Jesus Himself conquered, and with faith that He Himself is with us, to maintain the power and victory of His blood: then we also "are more than conquerors through him that loved us."

> ➢ **THIS VICTORY OF FAITH IS IN FELLOWSHIP WITH THE BLOOD OF THE LAMB.**

The Scarlet Thread

Faith is not merely a thought of which I lay hold, a conviction that possesses me, IT, Faith is a life. Faith brings the soul into direct contact with God, and the unseen things of heaven, but above all, with the blood of Jesus. **IT IS NOT POSSIBLE TO BELIEVE IN VICTORY OVER SATAN BY THE BLOOD WITHOUT BEING MYSELF BROUGHT ENTIRELY UNDER ITS POWER.**

Belief in the power of the blood awakens in me a desire for an: experience of its power in myself; each experience of its power makes belief in victory more carious.

Christians today need to seek to enter more deeply into the perfect **RECONCILIATION WITH GOD** which is yours.

Live constantly, exercising faith in the assurance that, "the blood cleanses from all sin;" yield yourself to be sanctified and brought nigh to God through the blood; let it be your life-giving nourishment and Power. You will thus have an unbroken experience of victory over Satan and his temptations. He, who, as a consecrated priest, walks with God, will rule as a conquering king over Satan.

If you are saved, our Lord Jesus by His blood has made us not only priests but kings unto God, that we may draw near to God, not only in priestly purity and Ministry, but that also in kingly power we may rule with God. A kingly spirit must inspire us; a kingly courage to rule over our enemies. *The blood of the Lamb* must increasingly be a token and seal, not only of **RECONCILIATION** for all guilt, but of victory over all the power of sin.

The Resurrection and Ascension of Jesus, and the casting out of Satan, were the results of the shedding of His blood. In you also, the sprinkling of the

Chapter Seven

blood will open the way for the full enjoyment of Resurrection with Jesus, and of being seated with Him in the heavenly places.

I once more, therefore, encourage each of you to open your entire being to the incoming of the power of **the blood of Jesus**, and then your life will become a continual observance of the Resurrection and Ascension of our Lord, and a continual victory over all the powers of hell. Your heart, too, will constantly unite with the song of heaven, "Now is come salvation, and strength and the kingdom of our God, and the power of his Christ; for the accuser of our brethren is cast down... They overcame him *by the blood of the Lamb*" (Revelation 12:10-11).

The believer who desires to share in the victory over Satan "through the blood of the Lamb" must be a fighter.

The Scarlet Thread

--- --- --- --- --- --- --- --- --- --- --- --- ---

SELAH!
THINK ON THESE THINGS.

The casting out of Satan from heaven is a result of the _____ _____ of _____.

Why did the Son of God have to come in the Flesh?
_____
_____

Because of the shedding of the blood of Christ that the Lord Jesus fulfilled the _____ demand.

How can we have a share in this victory?

1. There can be no victory without _____.
   How has your day been? _____
   _____
   _____

2. The victory of Faith is in the _____ with the blood of the Lamb. Faith is _____!

CHAPTER EIGHT

Joy in Heaven Through The Blood

Revelation 12:14-15

The Scarlet Thread

This explanation, given by one of the Elders who stood round the throne, concerning the state of the redeemed in their heavenly glory, is of great value.

It reveals to us the fact that, not only in this world of sin and strife, is the blood of Jesus the one hope of the sinner, but that in heaven when every enemy has been subdued, that precious blood will be recognized forever as the ground of our salvation. And we learn that the blood must exercise its power with God in heaven, not only as long as sin has still to be dealt with here beneath, but that through all eternity each one of the redeemed, to the praise and glory of the blood, will bear the sign of how the blood has availed for him, that he owes his salvation entirely to it.

If we have a clear insight into this we shall understand better what a true and vital connection there is between "the sprinkling of the blood" and the joys of heaven; and that a true intimate connection with the blood

Chapter Eight

on earth, will enable the believer while still on earth to share the joy and glory of heaven.

I. **IT IS THE BLOOD THAT BESTOWS ON US THE RIGHT TO A PLACE IN HEAVEN.**

It is clear that this is the leading thought in the text. In the question, "What are these which are arrayed in white robes and whence come they?" the Elder desires to awaken attention and inquiry as to who these favored persons really are and, as he himself gives the reply, we expect that he will surely mention what might be thought to be the most remarkable thing in their appearance. He replies to the question "Whence come they?" by saying that "they come out of the great tribulation." To the question, "Who are these?" (Revelation 7:14b).

That is the one thing to which, as their distinguishing mark, he draws attention. This alone, gives them the right to the place which they occupy in glory. This becomes plainly evident, if we notice the words which immediately follow: "Therefore are they before the throne of God, and serve him day and night in his temple; and he that sitteth on the throne shall dwell among them." Therefore, it is because of that blood that they are before the throne. They owe it to the blood of the Lamb, that they occupy that place so high in glory. The blood gives the right to heaven.

RIGHT to heaven! Can such a thing be spoken of in connection with a condemned sinner? Would it not be better to glory in the mercy of God only, who, by free grace, admits a sinner to heaven, than to speak of a RIGHT to heaven? No, it would not be better for then we should not understand the value of the blood, or why it had to be shed. We should also entertain false conceptions both of our sin and of God's grace, and remain unfit for the full enjoyment of the glorious Redemption which the Savior has accomplished for us.

The Scarlet Thread

The lack of this insight is sometimes found in the church where it might be least expected. I remember that while living in Tampa, Florida, when Marie and I had only been married for a few months, we were out on visitation and visited a home with an Asian lady and we did not have anyone on the visitation that could translate, and this lady, who had not the full use of her English, but whose heart the Spirit of God had enlightened to understand the meaning of the crucifixion of Jesus, with her finger pointed to her heart, folded her hands and then pointed to her palm, showing the blood had been shed for her sins.

The blood of the Lamb gives the believing sinner a RIGHT to heaven. "Behold the Lamb of God which taketh away the sin of the world." By shedding His blood:

- He really bore the punishment of sin.

- He gave Himself up to death really in our place.

- He gave His life as a ransom for many.

- Now that the punishment is borne, and our Lord's blood has really been shed as a ransom, and appears before the throne of God in heaven, now the righteousness of God declares that as the sinner's Surety had fulfilled all the requirements of the law, both as regards to punishment and obedience, God pronounces the sinner who believes in Christ to be righteous. Faith is just the recognition that Christ has really done everything for me; that God's declaration of righteousness is just His declaration that, according to the law and right, I have a title to salvation. God's grace bestows on me the RIGHT to heaven. The blood of the Lamb

Chapter Eight

is the evidence of this RIGHT. If I have been cleansed by that blood, I can meet death with full confidence I have a RIGHT to heaven.

Anyone that desires and hopes to get to heaven must listen then to the answer given to the question, "Who are they who will find a place before the throne of God?" They have washed their robes, and made them white in the blood of the Lamb. That washing takes place, not in heaven, and not at death, but here, during our life on earth. Do not deceive yourselves by a hope of heaven, if you have not been cleansed, really cleansed, by that precious blood and do not dare to meet death without knowing that Jesus Himself has cleansed you by His blood.

II. THE BLOOD ALSO BESTOWS THE MEETNESS FOR HEAVEN.

It is of little use for men to have a right to anything unless they are fitted to enjoy it. However costly the gift, it is of little use if the inner disposition necessary to the enjoyment of it is wanting. To bestow the right to heaven on those who are not at the same time prepared for it, would give them no pleasure, but would be in conflict with the perfection of all God's works.

The power of the blood of Jesus not only sets open the door of heaven for the sinner, but it operates on him in such a divine way that, as he enters heaven, it will appear that the blessedness of heaven and he have been really fitted for each other.

What constitutes the blessedness of heaven, and what the disposition is that is fitted for it, we are told by words connected with our text (Revelation 7:15). Nearness to and fellowship with God and the Lamb, constitute the blessedness of heaven. To be before the throne of God, and to see His face to serve Him day and night in His temple:

The Scarlet Thread

- to be overshadowed by Him who sits upon the throne;

- to be fed and led by the Lamb;

- All these expressions point out how little the blessedness of heaven depends on anything else than on GOD AND THE LAMB. To see them, to have intercourse with them, to be acknowledged, loved, and cared for by them, that is blessedness.

What preparation is needed for having such a relationship with God and the Lamb? Well it consists of two things:

1. There can be no thought of fitness for heaven apart from oneness with God's will. How could two dwell together unless they agreed? And because God is the holy One, the sinner must be cleansed from his sin, and sanctified; otherwise, he remains utterly unfit for what constitutes the happiness of heaven. Man's entire nature must be renewed, (II Corinthians 5:17) so that he may think, and desire, and will, and do, what pleases God; not as a matter of mere obedience in keeping a commandment, but from natural pleasure, and because he cannot do or will otherwise. Holiness must become his nature.

Is not this just what we have seen that the blood of the Lamb does? "The blood of Jesus Christ his Son cleanseth us from all sin." Where reconciliation and pardon are applied by the Holy Spirit, and are retained by a living faith.

- There the blood operates with a divine power, killing sinful lusts and desires; the blood exercises constantly a wonderful cleansing power.

Chapter Eight

- In the blood, the power of the death of Jesus operates; we died with Him to sin; so then through a believing relationship with the blood, the power of the death of Jesus presses into the innermost parts of our hidden life. The blood breaks the power of sin, and cleanses from all sin.

The blood sanctifies also. We have seen that cleansing is but one part of salvation, the taking away of sin. The blood does more than this; it takes possession of us for God, and inwardly bestows the very same disposition which was in Jesus when He shed His blood. In shedding that blood, He sanctified Himself for us, that we also should be sanctified by the truth. As we delight and lose ourselves in that holy blood, the power of entire surrender to God's will and glory; the power to sacrifice everything, to abide in God's love, which inspired the Lord Jesus, is efficacious in us.

The blood sanctifies us for the emptying and surrender of ourselves, so that God may take possession of us, and fill us with Himself. This is true holiness; to be possessed by, and filled with God. This is wrought out by the blood of the Lamb, and so we are prepared here on earth to meet God in heaven with unspeakable joy.

2. In addition to having one will with God, we said that fitness for heaven consisted in the desire and capacity for enjoying fellowship with God. In this, also, the blood bestows, here on earth, the true preparation for heaven. We have seen how the blood brings us near to God; leading to a priest like approach, yes, we have liberty, by the blood, to enter into "The Holiest" of God's presence, and to make our dwelling place there. We have seen that God attaches to the blood such incomprehensible value, that where the blood is sprinkled, there is His throne of grace. When a heart places itself under the full

operation of the blood, there God dwells, and there His salvation is experienced. THE BLOOD MAKES POSSIBLE THE PRACTICE OF FELLOWSHIP WITH GOD and not less with the Lamb, with the Lord Jesus Himself. Have we forgotten His word: "he that eateth my flesh and drinketh my blood abideth in me, and I in him?" The full blessing of the power of the blood, in its highest effect, is FULL ABIDING UNION WITH JESUS. It is only our unbelief that separates the work from the person, and the blood from the Lord Jesus. It is HE HIMSELF who cleanses by His blood, and brings us near, and causes us to drink. It is only through the blood that we are fitted for full fellowship with Jesus in heaven, just as with the Father.

Let this thought enter deeply into your soul the blood bestows already in the heart, here on earth, the blessedness of heaven. The precious blood makes life on earth and life in heaven one.

III. THE BLOOD PROVIDES FOR THE SONG OF HEAVEN.

What we have found out so far has been taken from what the Elder stated about the redeemed. But how far is this experience and testimony? Yes, they themselves bear witness. In the song, contained in our text, they were heard to cry with loud voice, "Salvation to our God which sitteth upon the throne, and unto the Lamb" (Revelation 7:10). It is as the slain Lamb, that the Lord Jesus is in the midst of the throne, as a Lamb whose blood had been shed. As such, He is the object of the worship of the redeemed.

This appears still more clearly in the new song that they sing, "Thou art worthy to take the book, and to open the seals thereof: for thou wast slain, and hast redeemed us TO God BY THY BLOOD, out of every kindred, and tongue, and people, and nation, and hast made us unto our God kings and priests:" (Revelation 5:9-10).

Chapter Eight

Or in words somewhat different, used by John in the beginning of the book, where he, under the impression of all that he had seen and heard in heaven concerning the place which the Lamb occupied, at the first mention of the name of the Lord Jesus, cried out, "Unto him that loved us, and **WASHED US FROM OUR SINS IN HIS OWN BLOOD**, and hath made us kings and priests unto God and his Father; to him be glory and dominion for ever, Amen." (Revelation 1: 5-6).

Without ceasing, the blood of the Lamb continues to be the power to awaken the saved, to their song of joy and thanksgiving; because in the death of the Cross, the sacrifice took place in which He gave Himself for them, and won them for Himself; because, also, the blood is the eternal seal of what He did, and of the love which moved Him to do it, it remains also the inexhaustible, overflowing fountain of heavenly bliss.

That we may better understand this, notice the expression: "Him that loved us and washed us from our sins *IN HIS OWN BLOOD*." In all our consideration about the blood of Jesus, we have had till now no occasion intentionally to stop there; and of all the glorious things which the blood means, this is one of the most glorious - - His blood is the sign, the measure, yes, the impartation of His love. Each application of His blood, each time that He causes the soul to experience its power, is a fresh outflowing of His wonderful love. The full experience of the power of the blood in eternity will be nothing else than the full revelation of how He gave Himself up for us, and gives Himself to us, in a love eternal, unending, incomprehensible as God Himself.

He gave Himself for us; He became sin for us; He was made a curse for us. Who would dare to use such language, who could ever have dared to think such a thing if God had not revealed it to us by His Spirit? That He really gave Himself up for us, not because it was laid upon Him to do so, but by the impulse of a love that really longed for us, that we might forever be identified with Him. Because it is such a divine wonder, therefore we feel it so little. But, blessed be the Lord! There is a time coming when we shall feel it, when under the ceaseless and immediate love-sharing of the heavenly life, we shall be filled and satisfied with that love.

It has been said that it is not desirable to lay too much emphasis on the word "blood;" that it sounds coarse, and the thought expressed by it can be conveyed in a way more in accordance with our modern habit of speaking or thinking.

I cannot share in this view. I receive that word as coming, not just from John, but from the Lord Himself. I am deeply convinced that the word chosen by the Spirit of God, and by Him made living and filled with the power of that eternal life whence the song containing it comes to us, carries in itself a power of blessing surpassing our understanding. Changing the expression into our way of thinking has all the imperfection of a human translation. He who desires to know and experience " what the Spirit says unto the churches" will accept the word by faith, as having come from heaven, as the word in which the joy and power of eternal life is enfolded in a most peculiar manner. Those expressions, **"THY BLOOD**," and **"THE BLOOD OF THE LAMB"** will make "THE HOLIEST," the place of God's glory; resound eternally with the joyful notes of "The New Song."

Heavenly joy through **THE BLOOD OF THE LAMB**: that will be the portion of all, here on earth, which with undivided heart yields to its power; and of all above, in heaven, who have become worthy to take a place among the multitude around the throne.

Chapter Eight

In this chapter we have learned what those in heaven say, and how they sing about the blood. Let us pray earnestly that these tidings may have the effect on us, which our Lord intended.

We have seen that to live a real heavenly life it is necessary to abide in the full power of the blood. The blood bestows the right to enter heaven.

May our life on earth become what it ought to be!!!!

"To him be the glory and dominion forever and ever." Amen!

The Scarlet Thread

– – – – – – – – – – – – – – – –

SELAH!
THINK ON THESE THINGS

The _____ gives the right to Heaven.

What constitutes the blessedness of heaven?
_____ to and _____ with God and the _____.

Can you remember the reference to the new song that we will sing in heaven? _____

Really praise God now for this truth: "**His blood** is the sign, the measure, yes, and the impartation of His love. Why not for a moment, just bow your head and **thank God** for the out flowing of **His wonderful love**.

CHAPTER NINE

Living in "The Holiest"
Through The Blood
Hebrews 10:19-22

The Scarlet Thread

"Having therefore, brethren, boldness to enter into the Holiest by the blood of Jesus, by a new and living way, which he hath consecrated for us, through the veil, that is to say, his flesh; and having a great priest over the house of God; let us draw near with a true heart in full assurance of faith, having our hearts sprinkled from an evil conscience, and our bodies washed with pure water" (Hebrews 10:19-22).

In these words we have a summary of the chief contents of this letter, and of the "Good News" about God's grace.

Through sin, man was driven out of Paradise, away from the very presence and fellowship of God. God in His mercy, from the beginning, sought to restore the broken fellowship.

To this end He gave to Israel, through the types of the Tabernacle, the expectation of a time to come, when the wall of partition should be removed, so that His people might dwell in His presence. "When shall I come and appear before God" was the longing sigh of the saints of the Old Covenant.

Chapter Nine

It is sad that many of God's children under the New Covenant who do not understand that the way into "THE HOLIEST" has really been opened, and that every child of God may, and ought, to have his real dwelling-place there.

The passage of this chapter gives us four words, what God has prepared for us, as the sure ground on which our fellowship with Him may rest. Then in a second series of four words, we see how we may be prepared to enter into that fellowship, and to live in it.

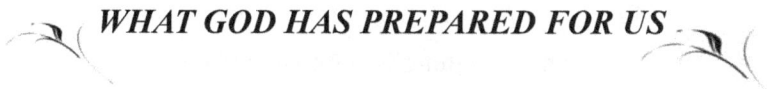

WHAT GOD HAS PREPARED FOR US

I. **"THE HOLIEST."**

"HAVING THEREFORE BOLDNESS TO ENTER INTO '*THE HOLIEST*' LET US DRAW NEAR."

To bring us into "*The Holiest*" is the end of the Redemptive work of Jesus, and he who does not know what "*The Holiest*" is, cannot enjoy the full benefit of Redemption.

What is this "Holiest?" It is the place where God dwells: "*The Holiest*," the dwelling place of the Most High. This does not refer only to heaven but to the spiritual "Holiest" place of God's presence.

Under the Old Covenant there was a material Sanctuary (Hebrews 8:2, 9:1), the dwelling place of God, in which the priests dwelt in God's presence and served Him. Under the New Covenant there is the true spiritual

Tabernacle, not confined to any place, *"The Holiest"* is where God reveals Himself (John 4:23-24).

One has said, "What a glorious privilege it is to enter into *'The Holiest'* and dwell there; to walk all the day in the presence of God. What a rich blessing is poured out there. In *'The Holiest'* the favor and fellowship of God are enjoyed: the life and blessing of God are experienced; the power and joy of God are found. Life is spent in 'The Holiest' in priestly purity and consecration; there the incense of sweet savor is burned, and sacrifices acceptable to God are offered. It is a Holy life of prayer and blessedness. Under the Old Covenant everything was material, the Sanctuary also was material and local; under the New Covenant everything is spiritual, and the true Sanctuary owes its existence to the power of the Holy Spirit. Through the Holy Spirit a real life in *'The Holiest'* is possible, and the knowledge that God walks there can be as certain as in the case of the priests of old. The Spirit makes real in our experience the work Jesus has accomplished."

As a Christian, you have liberty to enter, and abide in *"The Holiest."* As one who has been redeemed, it is a fitting thing for you to make your home there, and not elsewhere; for Christ cannot, elsewhere, reveal the full power of His redemption. But there, He can bless you richly. May it be the desire of our hearts to enter into *"The Holiest,"* to live in "The Holiest," to minister in "The Holiest." We can confidently expect the Holy Spirit to give us at conception of the glory of entering into a dwelling in *"The Holiest."*

II. THERE IS LIBERTY THROUGH THE BLOOD.

Admission to *"The Holiest,"* like *"The Holiest"* itself, belongs to God. God Himself thought of it, and prepared it; we have the liberty, the freedom,

Chapter Nine

the right, to enter by the Blood of Jesus. The Blood of Jesus exercises such a wonderful power, that through it a son of perdition may obtain full freedom to enter into the divine Sanctuary, *"The Holiest."* "Ye who sometimes were far off are made nigh the blood of Christ" (Ephesians 2: 13).

But that power could not be exercised for RECONCILIATION until it was first shed. By bearing the punishment of sin, unto death, our Lord Jesus conquered the power of sin, and brought it to naught by His death on the cross of Calvary. "The power of sin is the Law," by perfectly fulfilling the law, when He shed His Blood under its curse, His Blood has made sin entirely powerless. So the Blood has its wonderful power, not only because the life of God's Son was in it, but because it was given as atonement for sin. This is the reason Scripture speaks so highly about the Blood. Through the blood of the everlasting covenant God has brought again from the dead our Lord Jesus (Hebrews 13:20).

Through his own blood he has entered into *"The Holiest"* (Hebrews 9:12). The power of the Blood has entirely destroyed the power of sin, death, the grave and hell, and the power of the Blood has opened heaven so that we that are born again, by the blood, can freely enter.

How wonderful to know that we also have liberty to enter through the Blood. It was sin that took away our liberty of approach to God, and the Blood has perfectly restored to us this wonderful liberty. I encourage you to meditate upon the power of that Blood, appropriating it believingly for yourself and dear friend you will obtain a wonderful view of the liberty and directness with which we can now have an intimate fellowship with God.

The Blood pleads for us, and in us, with an eternal, ceaseless effect. It removes sin from God's sight, and from our conscience. Every moment we have free, full entrance, and we can have that personal fellowship with God through the Blood.

III. THERE IS THE NEW AND LIVING WAY.

"Having therefore, brethren, boldness to enter into '*The Holiest*' by the blood of Jesus, by a new and living way, which he hath consecrated for us through the veil, i.e. his flesh," the Blood bestows our right of entrance.

Jesus has shed His Blood for us: in that particular, we cannot follow Him. But the Way by which He walked when He shed His Blood, the rending of the veil of His flesh, in that way we must follow Him. What He did in the opening of that way, is a living power which draws and carries us as we enter "The Holiest of Holy." The lesson we have to learn here is this---the way into "*The Holiest*" is through the RENT VEIL OF THE FLESH and that was CHRIST'S death on the cruel cross.

One must remember that it was so with Jesus. The veil that separated God and us was the flesh. We also must remember that sin has its power over the flesh, and only through the taking away of sin, the veil may be removed. When Jesus came in the flesh, only He could remove that veil by dying; and so to bring power of the flesh and sin to nothing, "He offered up the flesh, and delivered it to death." This is what gave to the shedding of His blood its worth and power.

This is still true today that anyone who desires to enter "*The Holiest*" through His Blood must go through the rent veil of the flesh. We must realize that where the Blood of Jesus works powerfully, there always follows, the putting to death of the flesh. Anyone who desires to spare the flesh cannot enter into "*The Holiest*." The flesh must be sacrificed, given over to death.

Chapter Nine

In proportion as the believer perceives the sinfulness of his flesh, and puts to death all that is in the flesh, he will better understand the power of the Blood. The believer does this, not in his own strength, he comes by a living way which Jesus has consecrated; the life-giving power of Jesus works in this "way." The Christian is crucified and dead with Jesus, "They that are Christ's have crucified the flesh." It is in fellowship with Christ that we enter through the veil.

One author put it this way, "Oh! Glorious way," "the new and living way," full of life-giving power, "which Christ has consecrated for us!" By this way we have the liberty to enter into "*the Holiest*" by the Blood of Jesus. May the Lord God lead us along this "way," through the rent veil, through the death of the flesh, to the full life of the Spirit, then we shall find our dwelling place within the veil, in "The Holiest" with God. Each sacrifice of the flesh leads us, through the Blood, further into "*The Holiest*."

I. NOW LETS LOOK AT THE GREAT PRIEST.

As we get close to finishing this lesson and earthly tabernacle, what an excited truth that we have not only the work, but the living person of Christ, as we enter "*The Holiest*."

As seen in the Old Testament, the priests who went into the earthly Sanctuary could do so only because of their relationship to the High Priest; none but the sons of Aaron were priests. We have an entrance into "*The Holiest*," because of our relationship to the Lord Jesus. He said to the Father, "Behold here am I, and the children whom thou hast given me."

The Epistle to the Hebrews has shown us that Christ is the true Melchisedek, the Eternal Son, who has an eternal and changeless priesthood, and as Priest is seated on the Throne. He lives there to pray always; therefore also He is able "to save to the uttermost them that come to God through him." Yes, The great and all-powerful Priest.

Christ is appointed over the entire ministry of "*The Holiest*," of the House of God. All the people of God are under His care. If we desire to enter "*The Holiest*," then He is there to receive us, and to present us to the Father. The Scriptures are clear that Christ Himself will complete in us the sprinkling of the Blood. Through the Blood, Christ has entered, through the Blood, Christ brings us also in. Christ also makes acceptable our prayers, our offerings, and the duties of our ministry, however weak they may be. Not only this, but Christ bestows on us heavenly light, and heavenly power, for our work and life in "*The Holiest*." It is Christ who imparts the life, and the Spirit of "*The Holiest*." Just as His Blood procured an entrance, the sacrifice of His flesh is the living way. And when we enter, it is by Christ in whom we are kept abiding there, and are able always to walk well pleasing to God.

One has said, "just when it seems to us as if '*The Holiest*' is too high, or too holy for us, and that we cannot understand what the power of the Blood is, and how we are to walk on 'the new and living way,' just then, we may look up to the living Savior Himself to teach us, and to bring us Himself into '*The Holiest*.' He is the Priest over the House of God. You have only to cleave to Him, and you will be in '*The Holiest*.'"

With this taken care of, how can we be prepared to enter? Well, let's look at the answer.

HOW WE ARE PREPARED

Chapter Nine

It begins with a True Heart.

There are four demands that are made on the believer who wishes "to draw near." It is coupled with the second demand, "FULL ASSURANCE OF FAITH," and it is chiefly in its union with the second, that we understand what "a true heart" means.

The preaching of the Gospel begins always with repentance and faith. No one can receive God's grace by faith, ***if at the same time sin is not forsaken***. The full assurance of faith cannot be reached without "a true heart" a heart that is wholly honest with God and one that is **surrendered** entirely to Him. Let me interject, from my book, **Total Surrender, Walking by Faith,** "*that when one is committed, he or she is in control of what that commitment is for, but when one is surrendered, you are not in control, someone else is.*" "**The Holiest**" cannot be entered without "a true heart."

"Let us draw near with a true heart" (Hebrews 10:22). This is a heart that truly desires to forsake everything, to dwell in "The Holiest;" forsaking everything, to possess God. When a heart that truly abandons everything in order to yield itself to the authority and power of the Blood of Christ, that truly chooses "the new and living way" in order to go through the veil with Christ, by the denying of the flesh, then you have a heart that truly and entirely gives itself to the indwelling and lordship of Jesus.

Now that brings us to the question, who has a true heart?

"To draw near to God is an act of the heart or mind, whereby the soul, under the influence of the Spirit, sweetly, and irresistibly returns to God in Christ as its only center of rest. There is a constant improvement of the merit and mediation of Christ in every address made to the Majesty on high. The believer, as it were, fixes himself in the cleft of the Rock of ages; he gets into the secret place of the blessed stair, by which we ascend unto heaven; and then he lifts up his voice in drawing near to God, by the new and living way. He says with David 'I will go unto the altar of God, unto God my exceeding joy.' And if God hides His face, the soul will wait, and bode good at His hand, saying, 'hope thou in God, for I shall yet praise Him: He will command His loving kindness in the daytime, and in the night His song shall be with me.' And if the Lord smiles and grants an answer of peace, he will not ascribe his success to his own faith or fervor, but unto Christ alone" (Condensed from Eben. Erskine, 1733).

God desires truth in the inward parts, and therefore, "Son, give Me thine heart" (Proverbs 23:26) is His first demand upon us. Nothing short of this will ever satisfy Him. But more; there must be "a true heart:" a sincere, genuine, honest desire and determination to render unto Him that which is His due. We cannot impose upon Him. Beautiful language designed for the ears of men, or emotional earnestness which is only for effect, does not deceive God. "God is spirit; and they that worship Him, must worship in spirit and in truth" (John 4:24). How this condemns those who rest satisfied with the mere outward performance of duty, and those who are content to substitute an imposing ritual for real heart dealings with God! Oh, to be able to say with David, "with my whole heart have I sought Thee."

"In full assurance of faith:" which means, negatively, without doubting or wavering, positively, with unshaken confidence—not in myself, nor in my faith, but in the merits of Christ, as giving the unquestionable title to draw near unto the thrice holy God. "Full assurance of faith" points to the heart resting and relying upon the absolute sufficiency of the blood of Christ which was shed for my sins, and the efficacy of His present intercession to maintain my standing before God. Faith looks away from self, and eyes the great Priest,

Chapter Nine

who takes my feeble praise or petitions, and, purifying and perfuming them with His own sweet incense (Revelation 8:3-4), renders them acceptable to God. But let not Satan deter any timid child of God from drawing near unto Him because fearful that he neither possesses a "true heart" or "full assurance of faith." No, if he cannot consciously come with them, then let him earnestly come unto the throne of grace for them.

"Having our hearts sprinkled from an evil conscience, and our bodies washed with pure water." Here we have a description of the characters of those who are qualified or fitted to enter the Holiest. A twofold preparation is required in order to draw near unto God: the individual must have been both justified and sanctified. Here those two Divine blessings are referred to under the typical terms which were obtained during the old covenant.

"And our bodies washed with pure water," this figurative language is an allusion to the cleansing of the priests when they were consecrated to the service of God (Exodus 29:4). The antitypical fulfillment of this is defined in Titus 3:5 as "the washing of regeneration and renewing of the Holy Spirit." But here, the emphasis is thrown on the outward effects of regeneration upon the daily life of the believer. We need both an internal and an external purification; therefore are we exhorted, "let us cleanse ourselves from all filthiness of the flesh and spirit, perfecting holiness in the fear of God" (II Corinthians 7:1). The sanctity of the body is emphatically enjoined in Scripture (see Romans 12:1; I Corinthians 6:16, 20).

The whole of Hebrews 10:22 contains a most important teaching on the practical side of communion with God. While the first reference in the cleansing of the conscience and the washing of the body is to the initial experience of the Christian at his new birth, yet they are by no means to be limited thereto. There is a constant cleansing needed, if we are to consciously draw

The Scarlet Thread

near to the holy God. Daily do we need to confess our sins, that we may be daily pardoned and "cleansed from all unrighteousness" (I John 1:9). An uneasy conscience is as real a barrier to fellowship with Jehovah, as ceremonial defilement was to a Jew. So too our walk needs to be incessantly washed with the water of the Word (John 13). The Levitical priests were not only washed at the time of induction into their holy office, but were required to wash their hands and feet every time they entered the sacred sanctuary (Exodus 30:19-20).

It is just at this very point that there is so much sad failure today. There is so little exercise of heart before God; so feeble a realization of His high and holy requirements; so much attempting to rush into His presence without any previous preparation. "Due preparation, by fresh applications of our souls unto the efficacy of the blood of Christ for the purification of our hearts, that we may be meet to draw nigh to God, is required of us. This apostle hath special respect to, and the want of it is the bane of public worship. Where this is not, there is no due reverence of God, neither sanctification of His name, nor any benefit to be expected unto our own souls" (John Owen).

The new heart that God has given is a true heart. Recognize that. By the power of the Spirit of God, who dwells in that new heart, place yourself, by an exercise of your will, on the side of God against the sin that is still in your flesh. Say to the Lord Jesus, the High Priest, that you submit, and cast down before Him every sin, and all of yourself life, forsaking all to follow Him.

And as regards the hidden depths of sin in your flesh, of which you are not yet conscious, and the malice of your heart for them also provision is made. "Search me, O God, and know my heart." Subject yourself continually to the heart-searching light of the Spirit. He will uncover what is hidden from you. He who does this has a true heart to enter into "The Holiest."

Chapter Nine

Let us not be afraid to say to God that we draw near with a true heart. Let us be assured that God will not judge us according to the perfection of what we do, but according to the honesty with which we yield ourselves. Lay aside every known sin, and with which we accept conviction by the Holy Spirit of all our hidden sin. A heart that does this honestly is, in God's sight, a true heart. And with a true heart "***The Holiest***" is approached through the Blood. Praised be God! Through His Spirit we have a true heart.

IT CONTINUES WITH FULL ASSURANCE OF FAITH

We know what place faith occupies in God's dealings with man. "Without faith it is impossible to please Him." Here at the entrance into "The Holiest" all depends on "the full assurance of faith."

There must be "a full assurance of faith" that there is a Holy Place where we can dwell and walk with God, and that the power of the precious Blood has conquered sin so perfectly that nothing can prevent our undisturbed fellowship with God; and that the way which Jesus has sanctified through His flesh is a living way, which carries those who tread on it with eternal living power; and that the great Priest over the house of God can save to the uttermost those who come to God through Him; that He by His Spirit works in us everything that is needful for life in "***The Holiest.***" These things we must believe and hold fast in "the full assurance of faith."

The Scarlet Thread

Having described the threefold privilege which Christians have been granted, the apostle now points out the threefold duty which is entailed; the first of which is here in view, namely, to enter the Holiest, to draw near unto God, as joyful worshipers. To "draw near" unto God is a sacerdotal act, common to all the saints, who are made priests unto God (Revelation 1:6): the Greek word expressing the whole performance of all Divine worship, approaching unto the Most High to present their praises and petitions, both publicly and privately.

"To draw near to God is an act of the heart or mind, whereby the soul, under the influence of the Spirit, sweetly, and irresistibly returns to God in Christ as its only center of rest. There is a constant improvement of the merit and mediation of Christ in every address made to the Majesty on high. The believer, as it were, fixes himself in the cleft of the Rock of ages; he gets into the secret place of the blessed stair, by which we ascend unto heaven; and then he lifts up his voice in drawing near to God, by the new and living way. He says with David 'I will go unto the altar of God, unto God my exceeding joy.' And if God hides His face, the soul will wait, and bode good at His hand, saying, 'hope thou in God, for I shall yet praise Him: He will command His loving kindness in the daytime, and in the night His song shall be with me.' And if the Lord smiles and grants an answer of peace, he will not ascribe his success to his own faith or fervor, but unto Christ alone" (Condensed from Eben. Erskine, 1733).

"Let us draw near with a true heart in full assurance of faith." This is the requisite manner in which we must approach unto God. It is not sufficient to assume a reverent posture of body, or worship with our lips only; nor is God honored when we give way to unbelief. A "true heart" is opposed to a double, doubting, distrustful, and hypocritical heart. All dissimilation is to be avoided in our dealings with Him who "trieth the hearts and the reins" and "whose eyes are like a flame of fire."

Chapter Nine

God desireth truth in the inward parts, and therefore, "Son, give Me thine heart" (Proverbs 23:26) is His first demand upon us. Nothing short of this will ever satisfy Him. But more; there must be "a true heart:" a sincere, genuine, honest desire and determination to render unto Him that which is His due. We cannot impose upon Him. Beautiful language designed for the ears of men, or emotional earnestness which is only for effect, does not deceive God. "God is spirit; and they that worship Him, must worship in spirit and in truth" (John 4:24). How this condemns those who rest satisfied with the mere outward performance of duty, and those who are content to substitute an imposing ritual for real heart dealings with God! Oh to be able to say with David, "with my whole heart have I sought Thee."

"In full assurance of faith:" which means, negatively, without doubting or wavering, positively, with unshaken confidence—not in myself, nor in my faith, but in the merits of Christ, as giving the unquestionable title to draw near unto the thrice holy God. "Full assurance of faith" points to the heart resting and relying upon the absolute sufficiency of the blood of Christ which was shed for my sins, and the efficacy of His present intercession to maintain my standing before God. Faith looks away from self, and eyes the great Priest, who takes my feeble praise or petitions, and, purifying and perfuming them with His own sweet incense (Revelation 8:3-4), renders them acceptable to God. But let not Satan deter any timid child of God from drawing near unto Him because fearful that he neither possesses a "true heart" or "full assurance of faith." No, if he cannot consciously come with them, then let him earnestly come unto the throne of grace for them.

But how can I get there? How can my faith grow to this full assurance? We must have fellowship with "Jesus who is the finisher of faith" (Hebrews 12:2). It is important to remember that "The cloud of witnesses is not the object on which our heart is fixed. They testify of faith, and we cherish their memory with gratitude, and walk with a firmer step because of the music of their lives. **Our eye,**

The Scarlet Thread

however, is fixed, not on many, but on One; not on the army, but the Leader; not on the servants, but the Lord. We see Jesus only, and from Him we derive our true strength, even as He is our light of life" (Adolph Saphir). In all things Christ has the preeminence: He is placed here not among the other "racers," but as One who, instead of exemplifying certain characteristics of faith, as they did, is the "Author and Finisher" of faith in His own person.

Our text presents the Lord as the supreme Example for racers, as well as the great Object of their faith, though this is somewhat obscured by the rendering of the A.V. Our text is not referring to Christ begetting faith in His people and sustaining it to the end, though that is a truth plainly enough taught elsewhere. Instead, He is here viewed as the One, who Himself began and completed the whole course of faith, so as to be Himself the one perfect example and witness of what faith is. It was because of "the joy set before Him"—steadily and trustfully held in view—that He ran His race. His "enduring of the cross" was the completest trial and most perfect exemplification of faith. In consequence, He is now seated at the right hand of God, as both the Pattern and Object of faith, and His promise is "to him that overcometh will I grant to sit with Me in My throne, even as I also overcame, and am set down with My Father in His throne" (Revelation 3:21).

It is to be duly noted that the little word "our" is a supplement, being supplied by the translators: it may without detriment, and with some advantage, be omitted. The Greek word for "Author" does not mean so much one who "causes" or "originates," as one who "takes the lead." The same word is rendered "Captain of our salvation" in Hebrews 2:10, and in Acts 3:15, the "Prince of life." There its obvious meaning is Leader or Chief, one going in advance of those who follow. The Savior is here represented as the Leader of all the long procession of those who had lived by faith, as the great Pattern for

Chapter Nine

us to imitate. Confirmation of this is found in the Spirit's use of the personal name "Jesus" here, rather than His title of office—"Christ." Stress is thereby laid upon His humanity. The Man Jesus was so truly made like unto His brethren in all things that the life which He lived was the life of faith. Yes, the life which Jesus lived here upon earth was a life of faith. This has not been given sufficient prominence. In this, as in all things, He is our perfect Model.

As the great Priest over the house of God, He enables us to appropriate faith. By considering Him, His wonderful love, His perfect work, His precious and all-powerful Blood, faith is sustained and strengthened. God has given Him to awaken faith. By keeping our eyes fixed on Him, faith and the full assurance of faith become ours.

In handling the Word of God, remember that "his faith cometh by hearing, and hearing by the Word of God." Faith comes by the Word and grows by The Word, but not the Word as letter, but as the voice of Jesus'; only "the words that I speak unto you" are spirit-life, only in Him are the promises of God "Yea and Amen." Take time to meditate on the Word and treasure it in your heart, but always with a heart set on Jesus Himself. It is faith in Jesus that saves.

Remember that "to him that hath shall be given." Take use of the faith that you have; exercise it; declare it; and let your believing trust in God become the chief occupation of your life. God wishes to have children who believe Him; He desires nothing so much as faith. Why not get accustomed to say with each prayer, "Lord I believe that I shall obtain this." As you read each promise in Scripture say, "Lord I Believe Thou wilt fulfill this in me." The whole day through, make it your holy habit in everything-yes, everything-to exercise trust in God's guidance, and God's blessing.

The Scarlet Thread

To enter into *"The Holiest"* "full assurance of faith" is necessary. "Let us draw near in full assurance of faith." Redemption through the Blood is so perfect and powerful; the love and grace of Jesus so overflowing; the blessedness of dwelling in *"The Holiest"* is so surely for us and within our reach. "Let us draw near in full assurance of faith."

"HOW IS THE HEART CLEANSED"

Let us draw near, having **"OUR HEART CLEANSED FROM AN EVIL CONSCIENCE."**

The heart is the center of human life, and the conscience is the centre of the heart. By his conscience man realizes his relationship to God, and an evil conscience tells him that all is not right between God and himself; not merely that he commits sin, but that he is sinful, and alienated from God. A good or clear conscience bears witness that he is well pleasing to God (Hebrews 11:5). It bears witness not only that his sins are forgiven, but that his heart is sincere before God. He who desires to enter *"The Holiest"* must have his heart cleansed from an evil conscience. The words are translated "our hearts sprinkled from an evil conscience." It is the sprinkling of the Blood that avails. The Blood of Christ will purify your conscience to serve the true and living God. Here we have a description of the characters of those who are qualified or fitted to enter the Holiest. A twofold preparation is required in order to draw near unto God: the individual must have been both justified and sanctified. Here those two Divine blessings are referred to under the typical terms which obtained during the old covenant.

Chapter Nine

"Having your hearts sprinkled from an evil conscience." The Jewish cleansing or "sprinkling" with blood related only to that which was eternal, and could not make the conscience perfect (Hebrews 9:9); but the sacrifice of Christ was designed to give peace to the troubled mind and confidence before God. An "evil conscience" is one that accuses of guilt and oppresses because of unpardoned sin. It is by the exercise of faith in the sufficiency of the atoning blood of Christ—the Spirit applying experimentally its efficacious virtue—the conscience is purged. "Being justified by faith, we have peace with God" (Romans 5:1): we are freed from a sense of condemnation, and the troubled heart rests in Christ.

"And our bodies washed with pure water," this figurative language is an allusion to the cleansing of the priests when they were consecrated to the service of God (Exodus 29:4). The antitypical fulfillment of this is defined in Titus 3:5 as "the washing of regeneration and renewing of the Holy Spirit." But here, the emphasis is thrown on the outward effects of regeneration upon the daily life of the believer. We need both an internal and an external purification; therefore are we exhorted, "let us cleanse ourselves from all filthiness of the flesh and spirit, perfecting holiness in the fear of God" (II Corinthians 7:1). The sanctity of the body is emphatically enjoined in Scripture.

We have already seen that entrance to "***The Holiest***" is by the Blood, by which Jesus went in to the Father. But that is not enough. There is a two-fold sprinkling. The priests who drew near to God were not only reconciled through the sprinkling of Blood before God on the altar, but their very persons must be sprinkled with the Blood. The Blood of Jesus must be so brought by the Holy Spirit into direct contact with our hearts that our hearts become cleansed from an evil conscience. The Blood removes all self-condemnation. It cleanses the conscience. Conscience then witnesses that the removal of guilt has been so perfectly completed, there is no longer the least separation between God and us. Conscience bears witness that we are well pleasing to God; that our heart is cleansed; that we through the sprinkling of the Blood are in true living fellowship with God. Yes, the Blood of Jesus Christ cleanses from all sin, not only from the guilt, but also from the stain of sin.

Through the power of the Blood our fallen nature is prevented from exercising its power, just as a fountain by its gentle spray cleanses the grass that otherwise would be covered with dust, and keeps it fresh and green, so the Blood works with a ceaseless effect to keep the soul clean. A heart that lives under the full power of the Blood is a clean heart, cleansed from a guilty conscience, prepared to "draw near" with perfect freedom. The whole heart, the whole inner being, is cleansed by a divine operation.

"Let us draw near, having our hearts sprinkled from an evil conscience." Let us "in full assurance of faith," believe that our hearts are cleansed. Let us honor the Blood greatly, by confessing before God that it cleanses us. The High Priest will, by His Holy Spirit, make us understand the full meaning and power of the words "having the heart cleansed by the Blood;" the entrance to the Holy Place prepared through the Blood; and further, our hearts prepared by the Blood for entrance; oh! how glorious then, having the heart cleansed, to enter into, and to abide in *"The Holiest."*

"THE BODY WASHED"

Chapter Nine

Let us draw near, having the body washed with clear water.

We belong to two worlds, the seen and the unseen. We have an inner, hidden life, that brings us into touch with God; and an outer, bodily life by which we are in relationship with man. If this word refers to the body, it refers to the entire life in the body with all its activities.

The heart must be sprinkled with blood; the body must be washed with pure water. When the priests were consecrated they were washed with water, as well as sprinkled with blood (Exodus 29:4, 20-21). And if they went into the Holy Place, there was not only the altar with its blood, but also the laver with its water. So also Christ came by water, and blood (I John 5:6). He had His baptism with water and later with blood (Luke 12:50).

There is for us also a twofold cleansing; with water, and blood. Baptism with water is unto repentance for laying aside of sin, "Be baptized and wash away your sins." While the Blood cleanses the heart, the inner man, baptism is the yielding of the body, with all its visible life, to separation from sin.

So "Let us draw near, having our hearts cleansed from an evil conscience, and our bodies washed with pure water." The power of the Blood to cleanse inwardly cannot be experienced unless we also cleanse ourselves from all filthiness of the flesh. The divine work of cleansing, by the sprinkling of Blood, the human work of cleansing by laying aside sin, is inseparable.

Here we have a description of the characters of those who are qualified or fitted to enter the Holiest. A twofold preparation is required in order to draw near unto God: the individual must have been both justified and sanctified. Here those two Divine blessings are referred to under the typical terms which were obtained during the old covenant.

The Scarlet Thread

"Having your hearts sprinkled from an evil conscience." The Jewish cleansing or "sprinkling" with blood related only to that which was eternal, and could not make the conscience perfect (Hebrews 9:9); but the sacrifice of Christ was designed to give peace to the troubled mind and confidence before God. An "evil conscience" is one that accuses of guilt and oppresses because of unpardoned sin. It is by the exercise of faith in the sufficiency of the atoning blood of Christ—the Spirit applying experimentally its efficacious virtue—the conscience is purged. "Being justified by faith, we have peace with God" (Romans 5:1): we are freed from a sense of condemnation, and the troubled heart rests in Christ.

"And our bodies washed with pure water," this figurative language is an allusion to the cleansing of the priests when they were consecrated to the service of God (Exodus 29:4). The antitypical fulfillment of this is defined in Titus 3:5 as "the washing of regeneration and renewing of the Holy Spirit." But here, the emphasis is thrown on the outward effects of regeneration upon the daily life of the believer. We need both an internal and an external purification; therefore are we exhorted, "let us cleanse ourselves from all filthiness of the flesh and spirit, perfecting holiness in the fear of God" (II Corinthians 7:1). The sanctity of the body is emphatically enjoined in Scripture (see Romans 12:1; I Corinthians 6:16, 20).

The whole of Hebrews 10:22 contains a most important teaching on the practical side of communion with God. While the first reference in the cleansing of the conscience and the washing of the body is to the initial experience of the Christian at his new birth, yet they are by no means to be limited thereto. There is a constant cleansing needed, if we are to consciously draw near to the holy God. Daily do we need to confess our sins, that we may be daily pardoned and "cleansed from all unrighteousness" (I John 1:9). An uneasy conscience is as real a barrier to fellowship with Jehovah, as ceremonial

Chapter Nine

defilement was to a Jew. So too our walk needs to be incessantly washed with the water of the Word (John 13). The Levitical priests were not only washed at the time of induction into their holy office, but were required to wash their hands and feet every time they entered the sacred sanctuary (Exodus 30:19-20).

We must be clean, to enter into "***The Holiest***." Just as you would never dream of entering into the presence of the President of our United States, as my wife and I were when we had the privilege to be on the White House lawn with President Regan, unwashed, so you cannot imagine that you could come into the presence of God, in the Holy Place, if you are not cleansed from every sin. In the Blood of Christ that cleanses from all sin, God has bestowed on you the power to cleanse yourself. Your desire to live with God in "***The Holiest***" must always be united with the most careful laying aside of even the least sin. The unclean may not enter "***The Holiest***."

Listen, God desires to have us there. As His priests we must minister to Him there. He desires our purity, that we may enjoy the blessing of "The Holiest." That is, His Holy fellowship; and He has taken care of that through the Blood, and by the Spirit, we may be clean.

Let us draw near, having our heart cleansed, and the body washed with pure water.

"LET US DRAW NEAR"

The Holiest Place is open even for those in our congregations who have not yet truly turned to the Lord as well as those that have never heard the gospel that Jesus Saves, for them also the Sanctuary has been opened. The

Precious Blood, the living way, and the High Priest are for them also. With great confidence we dare to invite even them *"Let us draw near."* As you have been reading, I beg, I encourage you, draw near. Jesus Christ the High Priest over the House of God is a perfect Savior.

"LET US DRAW NEAR"

"Let us draw near." The invitation comes especially to all believers. Do not be satisfied to stand in the porch get all the way in. It is not sufficient to cherish the hope that your sins are forgiven. *"Let us draw near,"* let us enter within the veil, let us in spirit press on to real nearness to our God. *"Let us draw near"* and live nearer to God, and wholly take our abode in His Holy Presence, *"Let us draw near,"* our place is the innermost Sanctuary.

"Let us draw near, having our hearts sprinkled from an evil conscience and our bodies washed with pure water." Don't just stop here, let your heart in the perfect power of the Blood, lay aside everything that is not in accord with the purity of the Holy Place. Then you will begin to feel yourselves daily more at home in *"The Holiest."* In Christ, who is our Life, we are also there. Then we learn to carry on all our work in *"The Holiest."* All that we do is a spiritual sacrifice well pleasing to God in Jesus Christ. Brethren, *"let us draw near"* as God waits for us in *"The Holiest."*

Chapter Nine

"LET US DRAW NEAR"

As we close this study on such a beautiful, wonderful, powerful, subject let me challenge you and myself that the boldness to *"enter into the holiest"* which is spoken of in our text is not to be limited to the Christian's going to heaven at death or at the return of the Savior, but is to be understood as referring to that access unto God in spirit, and by faith, which he now has. Here again, we see the tremendous contrast from the conditions obtained under the old and the new covenants. Under Judaism as such, the Israelites were rigidly excluded from drawing nigh unto Jehovah; His dwelling-place was sealed against them. Nay, even the Levites, privileged as they were to minister in the tabernacle, were barred from the Holy of Holies. But now the right has been accorded unto all who partake of the blessings of the new covenant, to enjoy free access unto God, to draw near unto His throne as supplicants, to enter His temple as worshipers, to sit at His table as happy children.

The Scarlet Thread

SELAH!
THINK ON THESE THINGS.

How can we prepare to enter the holiest?

1. It begins with a true _____.

    Can you recall the passage of Scripture that teaches this?_____.
2. It continues with full assurance of _____.
3. How is the heart cleansed? _____
4. Can you quote Romans 5:1? _____

"LET US DRAW NEAR...

EVERY DAY...

TO SIT AT HIS TABLE...

AS HAPPY CHILDREN"

Chapter Nine

As one has so wonderfully said,

"Brethren, 'let us draw near' let us pray for ourselves, for one another, for everyone. Let 'The Holies' so become our fixed abode that we may carry about with us everywhere the presence of our God. Let this be the fountain of life for us, that grows from strength to strength, from glory to glory, always in 'THE HOLIEST' BY THE BLOOD."

The Scarlet Thread

www.ingramcontent.com/pod-product-compliance
Lightning Source LLC
LaVergne TN
LVHW091302080426
835510LV00007B/361